BETRAYED!

How You Can Restore Sexual Trust and Rebuild Your Life

Dr. RIKI ROBBINS

ADAMS MEDIA CORPORATION
Holbrook, Massachusetts

Published by
Adams Media Corporation
260 Center Street, Holbrook, MA 02343

ISBN: 1-55850-848-1

Printed in the United States of America.

J I H G F E D C B A

Library of Congress Cataloging in Publication Data
Robbins, Riki.
Betrayed! / how you can restore sexual trust and
rebuild your life / by Riki Robbins.
p.   cm.
ISBN 1-55850-848-1
1. Trust (Psychology) 2. Sex—Psychological aspects. 3. Betrayal—
Psychological aspects. 4. Interpersonal relations. I. Title.
BF575.T7R62   1998
158'.2—dc21   97-46386
CIP

*This book is available at quantity discounts for bulk purchases.
For information, call 1-800-872-5627 (in Massachusetts, 781-767-8100).*

Visit our home page at http://www.adamsmedia.com

This book is dedicated to my literary agent and dear friend, Susan Crawford, who has enabled me to rebuild my own life.

Contents

Acknowledgments

Special thanks go to my precious son, John, and my dear friends Rona Mendelsohn and Steve Raucher, who supported me emotionally during the aftermaths of my betrayals; Irwin Zucker, my publicist extraordinaire, who kept my career running smoothly during the worst of times; my brilliant teachers, Judith Sherven and James Sniechowski, who helped me understand the real meaning of intimacy; my talented colleague, Gera-Lind Kolarik, at whose rooftop swimming pool this book was born; my generous friend, Nancy Fuller, who gave me a safe, healing place to stay while I wrote the first three chapters; and Bill Barrett, who by his example has taught me how to trust again.

I am particularly grateful for the intellectual and intuitive gifts I have received from my mother and father, Harriet and Oscar Robbins. Their brilliant examples continually inspire me.

Helen Schucman and William Thetford, authors of *A Course in Miracles*®, have given me the answers to my spiritual questions. *A Course in Miracles*® is a nondenominational curriculum which has enabled me to create a new vision of the world based on forgiveness, love, and peace. The ideas represented in this book are my personal interpretation and are not necessarily endorsed by its copyright holder.

My love and warm appreciation to my friends and colleagues, who generously contributed their personal experiences, their wit, their wisdom, and their healing energy as this book evolved: Richard Adelman, Carol Adrienne, Nan Alimansky, Jane Ashley, Dave Ault, Monique Austin, P. J. Ballard, Brad Blanton, Jude Blitz, Barbara Bogard, Carlotta

BETRAYED!

Bradley, Jim Bridy, Eileen Broer, Armin Brott, Harold and Jeanne Brown, Ivan Burnell, Alexander Burnett, Richard Carl, Jan Carlson, Elsie and George Cedar, Lewis Chapman, Jama Clark, Bonnie Cohen, Susan and Forrest Craver, Ben Dean, Margaret and Alan Dolit, Patrick Douce, Danielle Draper, Ravi Dykema, Warren Farrell, Antol Feher, Marilyn Ferguson, Jim Floyd, Mikayla Forrest, Marc Freligh, Helen Friedman, Leah Garchik, Everett Gilbert, Norman Goldner, Steve Graham, Dee Gritzke, Louise and Ron Haine, Jacquie Hale, Steve Hall, Fred Hayward, Beth Hevda, Suji Hochenauer and Terry Fox, Burt and Bernetta Hoff, Maria Lucia Holloman, Kim Hunter, Cheewa James, Marie Janice, Bill and Matt Kayes, Chris Ketcham, Gerald E. Kiefer, Daphne Rose Kingma, Kathleen Kinsolving, Marty Klein, Rhona Konnelly, Joanna Levine, Dr. David C. Lewis, Chris Lien, Marty Lopata, Dennis Love, Peter Ludwig, Judy MacLeod, Karyn McNicoll, Mike Markarian, Kim Mason, Stuart Miller, Liz Mitchell, Jodie Morrow, Susan Murphy, Barbara Palosky, Will Pedem, Richard Pond, Jeff Raim, Steve Raucher, Carol Rhodes, Patty Ricci, Anita Rogerson, Carlos and Judy Roman, Diane Hira Rose, Franny Rosenberg, Shirley Runco, David Schiffman, Sandy Scholte, Pepper Schwartz, Shannon Seek, Jeff Seeman, Danny Seo, Paul Shaner, Jack Sherman, Judith Sherven and Jim Sniechowski, Amy Silverman, Sue Simmons, Sandra Slater, Judith Swack, Janet Tasker, Linda Tatum, Betty Ann Thompson, Bill Thompson, River Ulibarri, Doreen Virtue, Dottie Walters, Brian Washington, and Shohama Wiener. God bless you all.

Finally I acknowledge the excellent editorial assistance I have received from the staff of Adams Media Corporation, especially Ed Walters and Anne Weaver. It has been a pleasure working with you.

Author's Introduction

If you're reading this book, you've probably been betrayed. You don't need a collection of psychological case studies; you need help, understanding, and some sound practical advice. Rest assured, this book will give you all three. I'm not just standing there watching the goldfish being eaten by the piranhas; I'm one of the goldfish! So are all the other people who share their stories. We know what it's like to have your heart torn out. You are not alone.

The aftermath of a betrayal is horrendous. The lies, the disloyalty, the abandonment, the terror. Your face is covered with blood and the pain is endless. You've been knocked to the floor and you feel as if you'll never get up. But you don't have to take the betrayal lying down. Get to your knees and stand up. Now is the time to fight back, not to surrender.

I've felt the agony, the outrage, the helplessness, and the hopelessness, too. Yet I'm not bitter. I still have faith in God, in myself, and in other people. And I have more love and romance in my life than I ever did before.

In fact, betrayal can actually be a blessing in disguise. We can use what we've learned from our betrayals to create new relationships that are stronger, deeper, and richer. Eventually we may forgive our betrayer.

But it takes time. Right now all you feel is rage. That's normal. Before you can forgive you must fully experience your anger. Before you can find inner peace you must experience inner chaos. Before you can trust again you must confront your fears—and wrestle them, one by one, to the ground.

BETRAYED!
꒰꒱

All the people you are going to read about are real. Their names, occupations, and places of residence have been changed to protect their privacy. Perhaps you will agree with me that true stories are even more fascinating—and far more instructive—than fiction.

A final note: I'm using the masculine pronoun for the betrayer and the feminine for the person betrayed. If you are a man or a homosexual person reading this book, please shift the pronouns to fit your own experience. Whoever you are, I am reaching out to you in your agony and confusion to lead you back to love.

Chapter 1

How I Survived Betrayal

*M*y life has been a series of betrayals. Two major betrayals; a dozen or so disasters.

What do I mean by betrayal? According to the *American Heritage Dictionary of the English Language*, it is deception, disloyalty, or a breach of confidence.[1] In a love relationship, a betrayal takes place when one person promises the other to be sexually and emotionally faithful and then forms a secret relationship with someone else. The two may be having sex (not necessarily intercourse), exploring erotic fantasies, or sharing intimate feelings. The partner who betrays focuses his energy on the third person and on hiding what's taking place although he may be honest about the other details of his life. *There are two essential steps in a romantic betrayal: forming an outside relationship, and deciding to conceal it.*

When does your partner actually betray you? Not when he initiates the outside relationship. Remember, your partner *can* choose to tell you the truth about it. The moment he decides to keep the relationship a secret, the betrayal begins. Right now while you are reading this sentence, thousands of people are choosing betrayal instead of honesty.

Betrayals hurt. But I have learned that you can land on your feet— or on your head—depending on how you handle your experience. The advice I give you here, as well as in the rest of the book, can help you whether you're heterosexual, homosexual, or bisexual.

Here are my secrets of success (as well as the obstacles to it).

---

[1] *American Heritage Dictionary of the English Language*, New College Edition, Boston, Houghton Mifflin, 1976, p. 127.

TEN WAYS TO OVERCOME BETRAYAL—
AND TEN WAYS TO MAKE IT WORSE

1. *Preparation.* If you have noticed warning signs and are ready to deal with the betrayal when it happens, you have a definite advantage. *Denial* is deadly.
2. *Inspiration.* If you are inspired and feel powerful, you will act powerfully and decisively. *Powerlessness* is a self-fulfilling prophecy.
3. *Communication with the betrayer.* If you can talk to him, you have a definite advantage. If the betrayal takes a while to resolve itself, that also helps. A *sudden break* is much more difficult to deal with.
4. *Explanation.* When you know why the betrayal happened, you feel more in control. You can sort out your responsibility, your partner's responsibility, and the events that neither of you can control. If you *never know why* it happened, you stay in a place of confusion.
5. *Reparations.* If your partner is able to apologize and to make it up to you in some way, you'll feel much better. If either or both of you *are continually rageful,* you'll never get this comfort.
6. *Strong situation.* If you have lots of resources—good health, money, personal power, and spirituality—chances are you'll handle the betrayal well. If you *don't have resources,* you will find it much more difficult to rebound.
7. *Support foundation.* A network of family, friends, and sympathetic colleagues is essential. Children can also be superb supporters. Having a pet can help a lot. *Being isolated* keeps you from recovering.
8. *Emotional connection.* You need to be deeply connected to a few special people with whom you can share your feelings and experiences—even the ones you're most embarrassed about. *Loneliness* is bad enough when you're not being betrayed; it's terrible when you are.
9. *Sexual sophistication.* Knowing the joys and dangers of sex is a vital part of recovering from betrayal. You need to know how

to protect your body from disease if you have been sexually betrayed. You also need to know how to resume your sex life after you heal. *Sexual ignorance* can be painful—and possibly even fatal.

10. *Spiritual orientation.* If you have faith in God, a higher power, or a supreme being, it will see you through. I'm not saying you can't be an atheist or an agnostic, but *lack of faith* can defeat you.

My two major betrayals were like night and day. One happened when I was weak; one happened when I was strong. Notice how differently I handled each one.

Betrayed When I Was Weak

When I was the mother of three children, ages four and a half, three, and one and a half, my husband, Charles, left me. It was a complete and utter shock. I refused to face reality. After all, we had been married by a rabbi. Our marriage was a commitment for life.

When Charles walked out, I was physically ill and flat broke. After three pregnancies and four and a half years of lifting the children, I had seriously injured my back. I was still weak from the Caesarean section from my third child and the lack of sleep I had received since then. And there was no money, not even an emergency fund. All I had was ownership of half the house, some broken furniture, and a car that refused to start in the morning. Worst of all, I couldn't work because of the weakness and back pain. I didn't have my health, I didn't have enough money—and I didn't know how to recover them both.

Like a "good wife" of the sixties, I had given up my excellent position as a college professor and moved with my husband to a city where he could get a better job. My family and close friends were thousands of miles away, and I couldn't afford to call them regularly. From time to time they would call to check on me, but most of the time I managed by myself. Years later I met a woman who had lived a mile away from me whose husband had also left her with three children at exactly the same time. But I hadn't known of her existence. I never did have a strong support group to rely on.

I felt completely isolated. I didn't feel deeply connected with anyone, except the kids. Loneliness was a way of life with me. I thought I was the only person in the world enduring an agonizing betrayal. I believed that if other people knew the truth they would shun me. During the two years that followed, I signed Charles's name as well as my own on all my holiday cards. Finally a friend of mine confronted me. "Betrayal is as common as crabgrass," she said. "There's nothing to be ashamed of."

After the divorce, I hardly dated. I was afraid I might get betrayed again. Even though I longed for sex, I never had any. I was afraid of pregnancy, disease, and God knows what else. I made excuses to myself: the kids need me; women my age don't "date"; I'll meet men once my situation improves. I didn't know how to overcome my sexual fears, so they overcame me.

Betrayed When I Was Strong

This was not my last major betrayal. Many years later, while I was writing my second book, Negotiating Love,[2] unbeknownst to me, my husband, Buddy, began a relationship with another woman. When she called the house one evening, I questioned him carefully; he assured me that she was just a friend and there was nothing to worry about. I believed him. I had thought we had a clear understanding that if either of us were sexually attracted to someone else, we would tell each other. But he didn't.

Two years later he told me, "I'm leaving you for this woman. She's fifteen years younger than you are and has a young son; I've never had children of my own, and I want to help raise hers. It's a feeling I have. I just can't get them out of my mind."

This time I dealt with my betrayal very differently. For one thing, I had prepared myself for the possibility that I might be betrayed again. Also, there were signs that Buddy was interested in finding someone else and I had noticed them.

Immediately I began to focus on my mental attitude. As the author of The Empowered Woman,[3] I had given many seminars about how to

---

2. Negotiating Love, New York, Ballantine Books, 1995.
3. The Empowered Woman, New York, SPI Books, 1993.

manifest personal power. I knew that my self-esteem, self-confidence, and self-respect were the most important assets I had. I started believing in myself even more and surrounded myself with people who believed in me.

My faith in God had become a lot stronger since I had survived the first betrayal. A few years back I had started reading *A Course in Miracles*[4]; now I did one of the lessons almost every day. Its principles made sense. I became more and more sure that this second betrayal was part of God's plan for me.

I did all I could to make sure that there would be no sudden break. Buddy agreed to go to a few sessions of couple therapy with me; after he refused to continue, I continued our conversations at home. He wouldn't honor my request to wait six months before he left, but he was willing to spend time talking with me about how to deal with our situation.

At least this time I knew why I was betrayed. I was determined to have more information, so little by little I found out the details. The two of them had been seeing each other secretly while I had been traveling to promote *Negotiating Love*. Yes, I had been responsible for being less physically available, but the betrayal certainly wasn't all *my* fault. She was offering him something I couldn't give.

Once it became clear that he was leaving me for her, I was furious. But I also realized that if I unleashed the full brunt of my rage at him, we would be at war. So I vented—to my family, to my friends, and to my psychologist. I did have a couple of strong, angry outbursts, but on the whole I exercised self-restraint. Every day I prayed for the strength to continue talking and listening to him. My prayers were answered. Because we kept the lines of communication open, I was able to express my healthy anger and Buddy was able to express his remorse. What a blessing!

This time around I had lots of resources: I had my health; I had my career; I had my future earning power; I had half ownership of my house and full ownership of the furniture; I had my faith in God; and, most important, I had my strong belief in myself. My array of resources was no accident. During the previous three years I had spent time making myself physically, financially, psychologically, and spiritually stronger.

---

4. Helen Schucman and William Thetford, *A Course in Miracles*®, Mill Valley, California, Foundation for Inner Peace Inc., 1975.

Equally as important, I had created a support network of family, friends, and colleagues around the country. Somehow every time I was in despair, someone would write, call, or visit and restore my good spirits. And when I was feeling better, I expressed my appreciation. My most loyal supporters lived in my home. Every day, I received love, comfort, and companionship from my wonderful pet Chihuahua dogs, Fuzzy Bear and Spot the Dot.

Rarely did I feel isolated. Many of the people who called, visited, and wrote to me had betrayals of their own to share. As they talked, I realized that betrayal *is* as common as crabgrass. But few of us have the tools we need to cope with its emotional and practical consequences. And so this book was born.

Starting to date again wasn't easy. I didn't know how to say no to men I wasn't interested in, and I was reluctant to say yes unless it was someone I knew well. But I was determined to meet men; my betrayals weren't going to spoil my enjoyment of their company. If I wanted to be sexual, I'd send out signals. If I was ambivalent about having sex, I'd share my confusion. If I didn't want to be sexual, I'd manage to say no.

SURVIVAL STRATEGIES

I survived my second betrayal because I was aware of the difficulties I would face in its aftermath. Since your situation is unique, you need to develop your own survival strategies. As you focus on each of my secrets of success, ask yourself these questions:

1. *Preparation.* How much warning were you given? Did you have the opportunity to prepare yourself for the betrayal? Have you been developing your own friends, interests, and ideas instead of relying on your partner's? Are you able to prepare yourself to be financially, sexually, and emotionally independent right now? Are you willing to start?

2. *Inspiration.* Are you inspired to fight back instead of playing "victim"? Have you dealt effectively with other betrayals in the past? Have you coped successfully with other devastating situations? Do you consider yourself a strong person? Do you appreciate your own power? Do you know how to use it? Do

you believe that you can deal with the betrayal and emerge as a better person with an improved situation?

3. *Communication with the betrayer.* Is the betrayer willing to talk to you? Will he stay in dialogue with you while you explore your feelings? If not, can you communicate by mail or through a relative, friend, or colleague? Can you convince the betrayer to go to therapy, with or without you? Can the two of you sit down together and figure out a mutually satisfactory way to handle the effects of the betrayal on your children, your finances, and your sex lives?

4. *Explanation.* Will the betrayer share his reasons for the betrayal? Is he willing to discuss why your relationship collapsed and what the two of you can learn from the experience? If you can't get this information from the betrayer, can you find out what you need to know from other sources? If so, which ones?

5. *Reparations.* Is the betrayer genuinely sorry? Can he express these feelings of remorse to you? Will he listen to your feelings with empathy and appreciate your pain? Is the betrayer prepared to assist you in practical ways so you can emerge intact from the disaster? How will he help you with the problems he has caused you? Do you have the courage to ask for what you need—and expect to get it?

6. *Strong situation.* Exactly what is your situation? Are you physically and mentally healthy? What is your financial position? Are you able to work? If so, do you have a job or can you find one? If the job you have doesn't pay enough or is otherwise unsuitable, are you prepared to find another? Do you have children? Are they able to deal with the betrayal? How can they be of help to you? What other resources do you have to work with?

7. *Support foundation.* How may people can you count on to see you through this crisis? Whom can you call at 3:00 A.M. if you have a panic attack? Do you know the hotline number for your neighborhood in case you feel suicidal? Who will help you if you run out of money or get sick? Who will call regularly to check on how you are? Who will call occasionally?

8. *Emotional connection.* To which people do you really feel close? Whom can you level with about what's going on? Who's willing to listen to the gory details of the betrayal (in moderate doses)? Who will comfort you when you're weeping or screaming? Do you have a therapist? If not, do you know how to find one?

9. *Sexual sophistication.* If the betrayal was sexual, do you know how to protect yourself from its consequences? Have you gotten tested for HIV or sexually transmitted diseases? How are you going to handle your sexual feelings during and after the betrayal? How can you keep yourself from becoming numb, hiding out, or becoming promiscuous when you feel sexually vulnerable? How will you use contraceptives to stay safe once you're ready to become sexually active again?

10. *Spiritual orientation.* Do you believe in God, a supreme being, a higher power, or something else greater than yourself? Do you have faith that "everything is working for the good"?[5] Can you imagine that this betrayal is just another incident in your life and that the universe has a bigger, better plan for you?

I have been betrayed. You have been betrayed. Almost everyone we know has been betrayed at one time or another. Amidst our tears, let's reach out to each other, take each other's hands, and share our experiences. By talking about what has happened to us, we heal. As we listen to each other, we grow closer. When I empathize with you, I understand my own feelings better. Our conversation relieves our pain.

So let's get betrayal out of the closet once and for all. Telling our stories can make us free. Knowing how to deal with betrayal the next time it happens will strengthen us both.

[5.] Mary L. Kupferle, "Everything Is Working for Good." This pamplet, published by Unity School of Christianity, Unity Village, Missouri, kept me spiritually alive during my second major betrayal and still sustains me to this day.

Chapter 2

You *Can* Conquer the Pain

*W*hat was the worst betrayal you ever had? How did you feel? During both of my mega-betrayals, I was reeling from shock. Whatever my betrayer said to me, it hurt. (Both my betrayers kept saying, "I love you, but I want a divorce.") I felt my betrayers didn't care about me at all. How could they? *Watching someone fall apart isn't love. Not giving someone the attention she deserves isn't love. Wanting to be with someone else isn't love.* When the pain got excruciating, I finally said, "Enough please; I can't stand this anymore."

Betrayal throws you into emotional chaos. You feel as if there are a million bombs exploding inside your body. Your head aches; your heart aches. You can hardly figure out how you're going to get through the next minute, let alone the rest of the day. When I was going through my two mega-betrayals, I desperately wished I had a road map so I could have some understanding of what was happening to me. Now I finally have the map. It is my gift to you so you can conquer the pain just as I did.

Why Does It Hurt So Bad?

Only someone you care about can betray you. A casual acquaintance who doesn't show up for a lunch date may make you feel annoyed, but not betrayed. A salesperson who shows you a designer suit and then sells you an imitation doesn't make you feel betrayed. Ripped off perhaps, but not betrayed. But if your lover announces to you that he prefers someone else, you are devastated. If you find out that your partner is having an affair you feel as if your heart's beyond repair. Betrayal happens only with people you deeply trust and love.[1] You have a lot of emotional energy invested in the relationship. The more the person means to you, the more pain you feel.

Each betrayal brings up memories of previous betrayals. When I was betrayed the second time, I felt I was living my first one all over again. When Charles wasn't by my side when the children were small, it reminded me of how my father often wasn't there for me while I was growing up. If we have a long history of agonizing betrayals, a single incident can tear us apart.

Reach for a Healthy Voice

When you hurt you reach for a pill. Painkillers or tranquilizers may temporarily block out your pain, but they won't make it go away. Only listening to a healthy voice will heal you.

As a betrayal unfolds, you will find yourself experiencing five waves of painful emotion: shock, shame, sadness, rage, and outrage. During each of these stages, you will find yourself focusing on your negative feelings. Some of your thoughts will address how you are feeling: "I don't think I'll ever stop crying." Many will be about how you see yourself right now: "I feel like a total jerk." Others will be about your betrayer: "I'd like to tar and feather the idiot."

If there is no other voice to contradict your destructive thoughts, you will find yourself drowning in them. Your emotions will start to pull you down. You may be repeating affirmation such as "I am capable and lovable," but they won't help if you are still saying to yourself, "I feel like a total jerk."

What you need to conquer your pain is a new healthy voice that directly contradicts the destructive one screaming at you. Since this voice may not come naturally to you, you might have to write a script for it. Sometimes you might forget your lines, especially when the pain gets really bad. When everything you are hearing is destructive, you need to call a relative or close friend with a healthy voice and let her or him help you find your own again.

[1.] Marilyn Ferguson, phone interview with the author, August 11, 1996. Marilyn is the publisher of *Brain/Mind Bulletin* and the author of *The Aquarian Conspiracy* (London, Paladin Books, 1982).

Developing a healthy inner voice transforms you. The words you say to yourself affect how you feel. The words you say to yourself influence how you talk to others. The words you say to yourself determine how you behave. A destructive monologue—"I'm insane, my betrayer's nuts, and the world's falling apart"—will make you feel as if you are falling apart. You'll sound like a basket case to others, and you'll probably do more than your share of careless, even dangerous, things. A healthy voice—"I'm a good person and so is my betrayer, so let's figure out how we both can deal with this decently"—will make you more emotionally balanced, more articulate in sharing your needs, and more capable of going out and getting them met.

It is critical that your healthy voice be loud and strong before you talk to your betrayer. If you continually make statements such as, "I feel like a piece of garbage," your betrayer may treat you as if you were one. If all you say is "I hate you and I wish you were dead," you won't inspire him to be kind or helpful. What you say to your betrayer determines whether or not you emerge better off than you were before. You must start creating your healthy voice the moment you are betrayed.

The Five Pain Waves

You may experience the five pain waves of betrayal—shock, shame, sadness rage, and outrage—one at a time. Or you may experience several of these pain waves together. In either case you need to be able to recognize each one. Ask yourself these questions as soon as you start getting upset: How am I feeling inside right now? How is the world appearing to me? How am I seeing myself? How am I viewing my betrayer? It may help you to write your answers on a piece of paper while your emotions are still under control since you probably won't remember them when you're in agony.

THE FIRST PAIN WAVE: SHOCK

Shock is the first pain wave you will feel. After all, the betrayal happened all of a sudden. It's like an earthquake or a sudden illness; you just can't come to grips with it at the beginning. A nightmare has appeared out of the blue. And it doesn't seem as if there's anything you could have done to prevent it.

BETRAYED!

When you're in shock you feel totally confused. You will say things to yourself like "What's going on here? I don't understand what's happening to me" or "It's impossible—this can't be true." What's happening seems totally unreal. What you perceived as true isn't true. What you thought was love isn't love. When my apparently devoted husband Buddy told me he was leaving me for someone else, I said to myself, "Nothing makes sense. Night is day, and day is night. White is black, and black is white." I was gullible. I believed him when he told me, "I love you always." Now I know he didn't mean a word of it. How can I believe anything that anybody says anymore? Who is good? Whom can I trust? I don't know.

You start doubting yourself. You start questioning your own judgment—and you may even wonder about your own sanity. After all, you have just discovered that the reality you have perceived is false. You've been loving someone who has been treating you despicably. The truth was right under your nose and you didn't see it. You've been had. You wonder, "Am I a fool? Am I stupid? Am I completely naive? Do I need glasses? Is there something seriously the matter with me? Am I crazy, or what? Is he the same person I once knew or has he changed into someone else right before my eyes? Has he gone insane?" These questions really hurt. To admit that a person has betrayed you is to admit to yourself that there is a flaw in your judgment, which is really very difficult to do.[2]

Betrayal happens so quickly. It makes you realize, perhaps for the first time, the precariousness of life. What is here today may be gone tomorrow. What was true yesterday may not be true today. You ask yourself, "What can I believe in?" You answer, "Only the present moment."

Then you feel helpless. Until you were betrayed you may have believed you could control your destiny. Now you know you can't. In just a few moments the world has turned upside down. Your fundamental beliefs about life have been shaken up. You'll never be quite the same again. This is another reason why betrayal is so painful. You don't believe that you'll ever be able to take charge again.

[2.] Armin Brott, phone interview with the author, April, 1996. Armin is the host of the radio show "Positive Parenting" and author of *The New Father* (New York, Abbeville Press, 1997).

Now your healthy voice needs to intercede to help you along. Start saying these words out loud, every day, until you feel them work:

- *It really happened. I'm going to ask questions and find out what's going on.*
- *I'm not stupid, foolish, or insane. I'm a competent person to whom something terrible has happened.*
- *I may not be in control now, but I'm going to take control.*

THE SECOND PAIN WAVE: SHAME

Once you start facing reality, shame rears its ugly head. You feel completely embarrassed about the betrayal—as if you are the only person in the world who has ever been treated so badly. You find yourself saying things like "I'm so ashamed, I can't possibly tell anybody about what has happened." Right after Buddy told me he had been sleeping with another woman, I went to the hospital to get an HIV test. I felt as if a hundred eyes were staring at me as I walked into the waiting room. I made sure to tell the nurses very loudly that it was him, not me, who had cheated. "I'm a fool, but I'm not a slut," was my message. But at least my healthy voice was defending me.

You may also feel cheap. It may seem as if the betrayer used you as a means to meet his needs for sex, money, or a comfortable life. You weren't respected as a human being; you were treated as a commodity. When your usefulness ended he betrayed you. You were thrown away like a piece of old clothing.

Soon afterward you start feeling as if you're worthless. After all, someone has just treated you as if you aren't worth much. And you have been told that someone else is more valuable than you. I used to say to Buddy, "I guess I'll always be your second choice. I hear about how wonderful she is, not how wonderful I am." Ouch. During betrayal your ego takes a real beating. Typically your destructive voice says something to you like "I'm no good. I don't have much to offer anyone now." You also experience a lot of frustration. Feelings of hopelessness may overwhelm you, particularly when a relationship in which you've invested a great deal has just collapsed. You may think, "I gave my best and look what I got for it. I 'wasted' so much time and energy on this person. I gave so much love and look what I got—betrayed. Nothing I do ever succeeds. I can't ever seem to get anything I want in this world. Nothing will ever work for me again."

When you focus on your betrayer you feel that he manipulated and cheated you. You weren't given a chance to influence what he was doing. You had no say in the decision; your thoughts and feelings didn't count a bit. You feel your betrayer has excluded you from what's been really going on. You've been cheated of your right to know the truth. You may feel left out, just as you may have felt when you were a child (or a teenager). Eventually you just feel empty. You may think, "There's nothing left for me now. He's taken everything that mattered. I don't have much to offer anyone anymore."

Again, your healthy voice should now read from a brand-new script:

- *There's nothing to be ashamed of. I'm going to tell my friends and family all about what happened.*
- *It was an act of fate—something beyond my control.*
- *Our relationship was a worthwhile experience.*
- *I have much to offer to a new partner and to the world.*
- *I'm going to do something about what's happening right now. Let's see what strengths I have to work with.*

THE THIRD PAIN WAVE: SADNESS

Betrayal is often followed by abandonment. When you are betrayed, you may be deserted by someone precious to you. It's a terrible loss. Even if your betrayer doesn't pack up and leave, you still feel lonely and sexually needy. You feel sad from time to time; you may also feel depressed for days, weeks, or even months. Expect to have crying binges that start unexpectedly at any time. Eventually the weeping runs dry, although while you're experiencing it, you feel it's never going to end. You may tell yourself, "I'm so sad. I miss him so much." *Even though the betrayer has cut out your heart, you still feel a tremendous loss.* The pain of the abandonment is excruciating.

Whenever you notice something that reminds you of the betrayer it becomes unbearable. You counted on your partner, and now you feel completely alone. You may find yourself repeating, "Nobody cares about me. I'm so unloved. I don't make a difference to anyone's life. If

I died tomorrow, no one would miss me." (If you feel suicidal when you're in this mood, call a hotline immediately and also make an appointment with a therapist, psychologist, or psychiatrist.)

Here are some excellent lines for your new script, which will help you through your grief:

- *What can I do right now to make myself feel better?*
- *Who can I call who will cheer me up and give me love?*
- *Lots of people care about me.*
- *God loves me. I am never alone.*

Keep a list by your phone with the names and phone numbers of people you can call or visit when you feel sad.

THE FOURTH PAIN WAVE: RAGE

Rage, which is about injuring your betrayer, is different from outrage, which is about protecting yourself. You usually feel rage before you feel outraged. Your anger is out of control, and you are consumed with a desire to be verbally, emotionally, or physically violent. Attack energy consumes you; you find yourself screaming, yelling, name calling, even punching or hitting—perhaps for the first time in your life. You are furious at your betrayer. You think, "I'll destroy him. Just wait until I get my revenge."

You have fantasies of getting even with your betrayer. In your mind you tell him, "You'll be sorry someday. Your lover will leave and you'll come back to me on bended knees begging for forgiveness." Or even better, "You'll find out what it feels like to be cheated on. Maybe you'll lose your job and all your money, too. You'll get your punishment."

Whenever you feel that rage is about to overcome you, repeat these words:

- *If I do what I feel like doing, I'll pay dearly for it.*
- *Let's see how I can get angry with my betrayer without completely alienating him.*
- *Forgiveness will heal both of us.*

THE FIFTH PAIN WAVE: OUTRAGE

As you become aware of the injustice that has been done to you, your rage becomes outrage. Outrage is a call for action, the seed of your determination to fight back and get what you're entitled to. Your sense of self re-emerges as you realize how disrespectfully you've been treated. If you've been betrayed while married, you may start thinking of the lifetime commitment you have made to each other, which only one of you chose to break. Soon you feel righteously indignant: "How dare you do this. After all I've done for you, what nerve you have! This is so unfair."

This time your new script is similar to your old one:

- *I refuse to accept this inhuman treatment.*
- *I am sacred. I am worthy of respect.*
- *I deserve better than this.*
- *I'm going to do whatever it takes to get what I'm entitled to.*

Walk Through the Pain

No matter how much you're hurting, don't run away from your emotional pain. Don't be afraid of it and don't deny it; experience it fully whenever you can. Think of pain as your friend, not your enemy. It is the pathway to healing. You have to experience the full impact of each wave—shock, shame, sadness, rage, and outrage—before it will disappear. The more hurt you feel, the more completely you will recover from the betrayal.

Yes, your pain will become unbearable from time to time. While you're not hurting badly, be sure to find a therapist or psychologist you can call in an emergency. Discuss your pain with your medical doctor or holistic healer, who can prescribe or recommend some mild medication—but take this only when you really need it.

Talk about the Pain

The best medicine for emotional pain is talking about it. Your agonizing emotions will diminish quickly when you share them with a sympathetic listener. Letting out your feelings is good for both your mental and physical health. A heartache can cause your whole body to ache. If you hold everything inside, you'll probably experience muscular tension, headaches, stomachaches, backaches, and even memory loss.

Your pain is there for a reason. As you are going through all your emotional agony, you are being torn apart—and being put back together in a whole new way. You will emerge as a stronger, healthier person. It's surgery of the spirit. The process (which normally takes about a year) hurts, but the result is worth it.

The Bottom Line: Your Self-Preservation

As waves of emotion surge through you, you need to take care of yourself. Shock, shame, sadness, rage, and outrage are all painful, but your intention should be to feel good again. The shock, shame, and sadness linger for a long time. When you feel ready to let go of your rage, you know that you are starting to heal. You feel outraged at how unfairly you have been treated. You focus your energy on nurturing yourself instead of on punishing your betrayer. At this point you resolve to survive. You assess your resources and, if possible, you start working together with the betrayer for your mutual benefit.

Your healthy voice will start saying sentences like these:

- *Yes, I'm furious, but I'm not going to destroy myself.*
- *I'm going to use my anger to get what I need.*
- *I will not give up; I will overcome this betrayal.*
- *What can my betrayer do to make it up to me?*
- *Maybe I can turn this betrayal around and make it a positive experience.*
- *Let's see what I can learn from what has happened to me.*

Have faith in yourself—and your own future. As my psychologist[3] told me when I arrived at his office sobbing and screaming, "Whatever happens, you will get through this. There will be a brighter day." I didn't believe him then, but I do believe him now. I have conquered my pain, and you will conquer yours.

[3.] Ben J. Dean, Ph.D., clinical psychologist, Bethesda, Maryland. I am indebted to Dr. Dean for other words of wisdom sprinkled throughout this book.

Chapter 3

It's an Emotional
Hit-and-Run Accident

etrayal is an emotional hit-and-run accident. Suddenly your trusted spouse, love, or friend knocks you down, injures you, and possibly even leaves you. And you're in too much pain—or too embarrassed—to call for help.

Barbara, a college student attending a seminar of mine, was betrayed like this. She gazed at me forlornly and in a staccato, matter-of-fact tone told me the details. Her husband was having an affair, which Barbara had suspected for a long time. Finally in desperation she read his diary and found out the details. Soon afterward, he asked for a divorce and moved to a distant city where his "sweetie" is. He refused to talk to Barbara and wrote her a letter stating that he never wants to see her again. He didn't send her any support money, even though she is still in school. No husband, no communication, no money. How difficult it was for her to talk about her pain, even in a hushed whisper. "I am embarrassed by my embarrassment," she confided. But there is no reason for her to hide her head.

Betrayal can happen to anyone. It's an accident of fate, as common as crabgrass, but a lot more painful. *There is no stigma.* Almost everyone has been betrayed at one time or another.

If you were hit by a car would you keep it a secret? Of course not. You would have been injured. You would expect the culprit to confront you, to apologize to you, and to take whatever steps were necessary to repair the damage he or she had caused. If there were witnesses, you would expect them to come forward, validate your story, and testify on your behalf. Why should it be any different when we are betrayed? We should expect our betrayer to be held accountable and our relatives and friends to get involved.

You certainly wouldn't say to yourself, "The accident was my fault." Yet that's often what we do when we are betrayed. The truth is that the betrayal is *not* your fault. You didn't *necessarily* do anything to make it happen. You are a good person who has just had an accident. You were in the wrong place at the wrong time.

At the same time, you know that you may not be completely innocent. It is important to ask yourself, "Was I responsible in some way? How have I contributed to this betrayal?" By answering these questions honestly you may learn something useful. You may have made it difficult for the betrayer to tell you something you didn't want to hear. You may not have been paying enough attention to the relationship, so it didn't seem worth holding onto. You may have inadvertently created emotional distance or mistrust. You may have once betrayed your betrayer. Ask yourself these questions, but don't agonize. Remember, it's the betrayer, not you, who did the deed. He could have leveled with you about the problem, whatever it was, but instead he chose not to.

To blame yourself is wrong—and a waste of time. Your fury should be expressed to your betrayer, not directed toward yourself. You should be asking yourself, "What should I do now?" not "What did I do wrong?"

Another way to waste your energy is to vent your fury at the person who collaborated in the betrayal (whom I call "the accomplice"). Yes, you hate her. You envy the new relationship she has with your betrayer. After Buddy left I used to feel so jealous whenever I would think, "They're having sex while I sleep alone." It was mental self-torture. I made a conscious decision to think about something else whenever I started obsessing.

Asking yourself, "What does the accomplice have that I don't have?" will also drain your energy. The real answer is often, "Nothing." It may just be the novelty of a different relationship that is attractive, especially if the betrayer has been with you for fifteen years or more. Maybe the answer is "youth" or "maturity," "wealth" or "a simple lifestyle," "no children" or "children." In any case, you can't do anything about it. Getting a facelift, winning the lottery, adopting a baby, or sending the kids to grandma's isn't going to reverse the betrayal. Trust has already been shattered.

Besides, you can't undo a betrayal. A month after a friend of mine was diagnosed with lung cancer, her lover left her. He found her disease "upsetting." After she had healed he wanted to resume their relationship. But she didn't want him back anymore.

Instead of hiding out, indulging in recriminations, or trying to undo what happened, *you want to start asking questions as soon as you are betrayed.* Ask questions like these:

- *How will I feel during the aftermath of the betrayal?*
- *How can I cope? What resources do I need to get myself through?*
- *How do I deal with my betrayer?*
- *Can I ever trust my betrayer again? What about other people?*
- *Were there warning signs I just didn't see?*
- *How can I keep myself from being betrayed in the future?*
- *Where is God in all this? Can I trust in God again?*

Betraying Yourself

When you think about being betrayed, you picture someone else as the betrayer. Actually, the most devastating betrayals are those you do to yourself. You promise yourself that you'll lose twenty pounds, quit smoking, exit your dead-end job, or stop screaming at your husband every time you get PMS—and you don't. When you aren't true to yourself, you betray yourself.

To betray yourself is to destroy your spirit. By breaking your word to yourself you violate your integrity, the core of your being. How can you trust yourself then? When you don't take proper care of yourself physically, emotionally, or financially, you also abandon your best interests. You know you should go on a diet, throw away your cigarettes, or start job-hunting—but you don't. That's self-sabotage. It's much more destructive than a betrayal by another person.

Recognizing Betrayal

Most betrayals, however, are done by someone else. These include:

- *Sexual infidelity (cheating).* You promised you'd have sex only with me but now you're being sexual with someone else.

- *Metamorphosis.* I thought you'd always be the same person but now you've completely changed.
- *Domestic violence.* I thought you'd never abuse me but now you've turned into a monster.
- *Divorce.* You promised you'd stay married to me, but now you want "out."

WHAT IS CHEATING?

Sexual infidelity, which is often called *cheating*, is the most common betrayal. A person who has promised to have sex only with his partner has sex with someone else. What do I mean by "has sex"? Not just sexual intercourse, but any kind of intense erotic, emotional, or fantasy experience in which there is powerful shared energy. These include:

- *Extended foreplay*
- *Phone sex*
- *Cybersex (I call this "cyberinfidelity")*
- *Fantasy sex (viewing pornography as well as sharing and acting out sexual fantasies)*

Dr. Marty Klein, sex therapist and author of *Your Sexual Secrets*, tells this anecdote: "A client comes to me and tells me he is upset because his wife is fantasizing about Mel Gibson while they are having sex. I ask him, 'Which would you prefer: that she have sex with you and fantasize about Mel Gibson or that she have sex with Mel Gibson and fantasize about you?'" Needless to say the client preferred the former. But he still wasn't happy about what was going on. His wife *was* cheating on him; she had just chosen a way to do it that was less threatening.[1]

Your partner can cheat without going "all the way." If it happens once and you find out, you may be willing to overlook it. If it happens regularly, then you've got a full-blown case of sexual infidelity on your hands.

Cheating is a devastating betrayal. It's not so much because of the sex but because of what the sex represents: not keeping a promise. In addition

---

[1.] Conversation with the author, September 23, 1996 (*Your Sexual Secrets*, New York, Berkley Books, 1990).

to having sex (along with emotional intimacy and/or erotic fantasy), the betrayer engages in a deliberate deception. Withholding information, distorting facts, and minimizing the importance of what's happening are all breaches of trust. By carelessly disregarding a cherished agreement, the betrayer is shattering the foundation of faith on which the relationship has been built.

A couple can poorly communicate, argue, or even ignore each other and stay together—as long as they are faithful. When this understanding ends, the relationship is in crisis.

Dr. Pepper Schwartz, sociologist and author of *Peer Marriage*, tells a story about her mother, who has been happily married for fifty years. Dr. Schwartz had once asked her mother, "If forty years ago you had found out that Dad had been unfaithful would you have left him?" "Absolutely, yes," her mother replied. "It would have meant that everything was a lie." What she was saying was this: For ten years I had faith that my husband was who he proclaimed to be, I believed what he said, and I relied on him to be loyal. By cheating he would have destroyed *both* sexual exclusivity *and* honesty, the fundamental basis of our marriage.[2]

ONE POINT OF VIEW: CHEATING IS ABSOLUTELY WRONG

It's easy to condemn cheating, especially when you're the one who's been hurt. Cheating is unfair and immoral. Your sexual betrayer makes a premeditated choice to deceive the most important person in his life—you. Without consulting you, he creates a new scenario on his terms. Instead of openly declaring his intentions, he prefers to lay the groundwork for an easy out when he's ready to leave. It's a macabre plot deliberately designed to facilitate his escape and to embarrass you.

If your partner is very unhappy in your relationship, does he have the right to leave? Yes. Does he have the right to do it secretly? No. He has a duty to tell you how he feels, go into counseling, and spend at least six months working together with you to see if it's possible to keep your relationship alive.

[2.] Anecdote told at the special evening panel "Why Is Monogamy So Damned Hard?" of the Annual Conference of the Western Region of the Society for the Scientific Study of Sexuality, April 3, 1997 (*Peer Marriage*, New York, The Free Press, 1994).

Traitors who deliberately betray their country are punished with death. What about people who betray their partners—and their children? Shouldn't they suffer, too? Don't we have a responsibility to resist the temptation of sex even when it stares us in the face? Shouldn't we have a clear understanding that each of us has areas of privacy but no big secrets?

ANOTHER POINT OF VIEW: YOU SET YOUR OWN LIMITS

When I told a male friend of mine, a well-known radio talk show host, about what had happened between Buddy and me, he replied, "I can see your side but I can see his side, too. Buddy must have had good reasons or else he wouldn't have done it." At first I was shocked at my friend's reaction. Then I thought about it. Perhaps what he really meant was, There but for the grace of God go I. Haven't I ever betrayed someone? If we condemn Buddy, doesn't that mean I've also committed an unpardonable sin? He did mean that—and more.

My friend refused to judge either of us. He advised me to do my best to understand why the incident had happened, to repair the damage that had been done, and eventually to forgive and move on. At the time his suggestions sounded preposterous. It took me six months to realize they were guidelines for rebuilding my life.

Many betrayed people do stay with their partner. Some of them continue to harbor resentment; others manage to forgive—if not forget. And a substantial number overlook the incident completely, especially if it was a mini-betrayal.

Each of us has our own limits as to what we will put up with in a relationship. You draw a line in the sand defining what you will and will not tolerate. When your partner crosses that line you say to him, "This is unacceptable to me. I simply won't allow you to do this." When it comes to sexual infidelity, it is up to *you* to decide exactly what your limits are. They're uniquely yours. For example, "If you ever cheat we're through" or "One-night stands are okay when you're out of town" or "I don't mind secret cybersex as long as I get what *I* need." It's a good idea to share your limits with your partner—or you may discover them only *after* you have been betrayed.

METAMORPHOSIS: ARE YOU CRAZY OR HAS YOUR PARTNER CHANGED?

Sexual infidelity and divorce are clear cases of betrayal, but metamorphosis is not. When someone you love suddenly becomes a different person, at first you don't even realize you've been betrayed. That's why it's especially difficult to deal with a metamorphosis. You just can't believe what's happened.

DOMESTIC VIOLENCE: YOUR PARTNER BECOMES A MONSTER

Domestic violence is the most common metamorphosis. Here's a typical case: Carla, an elementary school teacher, married a man who was a model husband. He treated her well until their son was born; from that moment on he started to beat her. It was a complete surprise; all of a sudden her butterfly has become a caterpillar. Since she and her husband were both "pillars of the community," she was too embarrassed to tell anyone or to get help. Finally God intervened. She was in an auto accident and her physician sent her to physical therapy. The therapist kept saying to her, "I know you're hiding something." Carla revealed her betrayal and subsequently left her husband. Carla didn't deal effectively with her betrayal initially because she couldn't believe it had actually occurred.

Always be prepared for the possibility that your beloved may change. Events beyond our control may bring out a side of our partner we have never seen. Carla's father-in-law had beaten her husband and his mother when her husband was a child. Had Carla known about her husband's history, she might have anticipated his betrayal—or else decided not to have children until he sought counseling.

DIVORCE AND DEATH: FOCUS ON ABANDONMENT

When you and your partner get divorced, you may feel more abandoned than betrayed. Like it or not, suddenly you are living entirely on your own. The practical details can be overwhelming, and they're all you can think about. But at some point, preferably early on, you must deal with the betrayal itself. Otherwise your unresolved feelings will resurface when you're ready to form another romantic relationship. This will make it difficult for you to trust again.

Mega-Betrayals and Mini-Betrayals

You know you've had a *mega-betrayal* when you feel as if you've been run over by a truck. Your fiancé breaks your engagement; your lover runs off with someone else; you find out that your spouse has been having an affair. The whole relationship dissolves and you are abandoned. It's irreversible, not temporary. You will heal, but you'll never be the same. No matter how strong you are, mega-betrayals send you crashing to the ground. You need emergency first aid right away.

For example, Ellen, an interior decorator, is extremely attractive. When she was four months pregnant, her husband left her for another woman. She lost all her self-confidence, neglected her appearance, and went into a major depression. Gretchen, a construction worker, is highly respected for holding her own in a mainly male profession. Six months after her seventeen-year-old daughter died, her husband left her and ran off with a girl their daughter's age. Now Gretchen can't even get out of bed.

Mini-betrayals are painful, but they don't knock you flat. You gain back the thirty pounds you lost; your lover doesn't keep his promise to stop smoking; your spouse tells you he's working late and you find out he's going to bars instead. Breaking a promise is less serious than living a lie. Plus you're usually not abandoned after a mini-betrayal; the person sticks around and the two of you have to live with its consequences. You experience the five emotional waves, but they're less painful and don't last nearly as long.

While a single mini-betrayal doesn't destroy you, repeated ones can. It's like water dripping on a rock. A husband who always promises to call if he's going to be late and never does; a lover who repeatedly says he's sending flowers but they never arrive; or a husband who hints about great sex but is always busy when you approach him will eventually erode your trust. An accumulation of daily mini-betrayals can be as painful as a mega-one.

Real Betrayals and Perceived Betrayals

Most betrayals are genuine breaches of confidence. You believe in your lover's good intention to be sexually faithful; you have faith that your spouse will honor his marital vows; you rely on yourself to act in your own best interest. But sometimes when you feel you've been betrayed, you haven't been. The other person may have promised one thing, you thought he said another.

Ida, a legal secretary, meets Raoul, a construction worker, with whom she falls in love. Together they decide to have a sexually exclusive relationship. One day Ida goes over to Raoul's apartment and sees him in his car kissing another woman. When Ida asks Raoul for an explanation, he replies, "Yes we were kissing, but that's not the same as having sex."

Whenever you have an understanding with someone it's important to get clear on exactly what it means to each of you.

Betrayal Is about Loss of Trust

When you're standing on the corner about to cross the street, do you expect to be hit by a car? No. You trust that you're reasonably safe on the sidewalk. Drivers won't deliberately knock you down; pedestrians won't intentionally bump into you. If you believed otherwise, how could you comfortably stand there on the pavement?

It's the same in a relationship. You expect a person you love to keep his promises. You trust him to keep his word and not to deliberately hurt you, use you, abuse you, or take advantage of you.

Does your betrayer mean to destroy your trust? Maybe yes, maybe no. Some people simply don't care. Others intend to be trustworthy, but they're afraid to reveal their feelings—or their deeds. Afraid of a confrontation, they keep putting it off. When Buddy told me he loved me during our first ten years together, he meant it. Then his feelings gradually diminished. Rather than telling me, he kept on saying, "I love you, you're my most special person," all the time he was having the affair. After two years of this behavior, I could never trust him again to mean what he said.

Betrayal Is about Being Let Down

When someone breaks a promise to you, you are betrayed. We all know people who break their marriage vows: "I promised to stay with you 'in sickness and in health, for richer and for poorer, for better or for worse until death do us part.' Now I want to marry someone else." That's betrayal. When you trust someone you have confidence they will keep their word.

You know you've been betrayed when you find yourself repeating one or more phrases like these:

- *I relied on you to be my friend.*
- *I counted on you to be there for me.*
- *I believed that you loved me.*
- *I had faith that you would be honest with me.*
- *I thought you would tell me if something was wrong.*
- *I was sure you were faithful to me.*
- *I was confident you valued our relationship as much as I did.*

You sound like a broken compact disk, saying these phrases over and over again. But you can't help yourself. You've had a huge disappointment. You gave so much time and energy to this person. You expected love, friendship, trust, support, and respect in return. What did you receive? Lies, hypocrisy, abuse, disrespect, and probably abandonment.

Betrayal Is about Disloyalty

The essence of betrayal is disloyalty. The betrayer takes sides with someone else besides you, puts another person's interests ahead of yours, or worst of all connives with a third party against you.

Loyalty is precious. Who gets your highest loyalty? Yourself? Your spouse or lover? Your child? Your best friend? God? If your spouse's reputation is challenged will you stand by him? If your lover calls you at 3:00 A.M., desperately upset, will you stay on the phone even if it means missing an important meeting the next day? Or is loyalty to yourself more important? Conversely, when you're in a crisis, who will stand by you? Most of us have only a handful of people we can count on. An ally through thick and thin has a powerful hold on your life. Someone who will side with you against your betrayer is more precious than platinum. The two of you have a deep loyalty that neither is likely to betray.

Who is number one with you? This is one of the most important decisions you ever make. It's conscious and it's deliberate. When you give your loyalty, you put one person first, another second, another third. You can't give a little bit of loyalty to each one. You have to decide your priorities. If your house were on fire, whom would you carry out with you (assuming it could only be one person)? This will give you an idea of where your highest loyalty lies. When you get married you expect that your spouse will be loyal first and foremost to you. If there is a choice between you and someone else, you will always be number one. Epidemic divorce and sexual infidelity indicate that in many cases "it just ain't so" anymore.

Betrayers are consenting adults. Each one makes a voluntary and premeditated choice about loyalty. There are no accidental betrayals. Freely and consciously the betrayer decides where his best energy is going to go. Never mind about *your* feelings; he is concerned with what *he* needs. If you're hurt by the decision, that's too bad. He is actually saying, "A choice has to be made between taking care of your needs and taking care of mine. And I choose mine."

The worst kind of betrayal is divided loyalty. The betrayer gives and withdraws loyalty first to you and then to someone else. The man who leaves his wife for his mistress, marries her, and then goes back to his wife is a double-betrayer. So is the husband who says to his wife, "I love you—and I also love the other woman I'm sleeping with. I want to have you both."

Divided loyalty is confusing to the betrayer and agonizing to you. The betrayer is intimately involved with two people and can't level with either one. He feels as if he's been cut in half. As one man said to me who was caught between his wife and his mistress, "I'm going to have to pick one of them to be loyal to; otherwise I'll get caught in the middle and end up betraying both of them. Then I'll have neither."

The antidote to disloyalty is living in integrity. Now you are whole, giving your loyalty to one person, not dividing it between two. If your loyalty changes, you share this information honestly with your partner.

Betrayal Is about Lies

In *The Road Less Traveled*, M. Scott Peck talks about black lies and white lies. Black lies are sins of distortion (saying you didn't do it when you really did). White lies are sins of omission (deciding not to mention it). Betrayers tell both. They also lie in various shades of gray.[3]

Betrayers tend to think that white lies don't matter: "Never mind that I stayed out late and didn't tell you where I was." "It doesn't matter that I never explained that fifty dollar charge for flowers (that you never received) on our credit card bill." But white lies have a special insidious power. As they accumulate they increase in power and darken. We can create an imaginary equation: Three white lies equal one gray lie and six white lies equal one black lie. Whatever the exact numbers, one fact remains: The more you omit, the more you betray.

Lies multiply. Your betrayer has told a white lie; soon he has to cover it with a fib. Next he tells you a gray lie and then a black one. As one of my betrayers said to me, "Since I've lied to you so much already, there's no point in telling you the truth." Before you know it, the two of you are living a lie. You wouldn't recognize the truth if he told it to you.

If you have been betrayed, you've probably been lied to. Eventually you wonder, "Where do the lies stop and where does the truth begin?" In a mega-betrayal there is a whole web of lies. You move further and further toward complete mistrust. Since you can't rely on the betrayer's integrity, a healthy relationship is now impossible.

Lies make both of you miserable. When the betrayer pretends to be what he is not, your life together becomes hypocrisy. Initially, you know something is wrong, but you don't know what it is and are afraid to ask. So you hide your feelings. Your betrayer fears being discovered and hides *his* feelings. Both of you are living a nightmare. During the period before each of my mega-betrayals, I felt like an actress in a horrendous play that I didn't write. We would find ourselves discussing current events instead of where he had been the night before. It was mental hell. All I could do was go through the motions of living. When the betrayals were revealed, it was a huge relief. At least the truth was out.

The antidote to lying is honesty. As Gestalt psychologist and seminar leader Dr. Brad Blanton writes, you start telling yourself the whole truth instead of avoiding what's unpleasant. As you get more comfortable with

---

[3.] *The Road Less Traveled*, New York, Simon & Schuster, 1978.

your real self you become less concerned about "looking good" to others. You become more open and authentic instead of hiding behind a wall of misinformation. Your relationships become peak experiences instead of empty charades.[4]

Betrayal Is about Love

Jane, an entrepreneur, married the man of her dreams. He had two children who rejected her and verbally abused her. Although he loved Jane very much, he took his children's side. She was devastated. Holding hands and weeping together, they went to three different psychotherapists and told their story. No one helped them. Without warning, Jane left him, her stepchildren, and their five-million-dollar business so she could psychologically survive.

You can love somebody and still betray them. This is the most painful kind of betrayal. My former husbands were both good, kind men. They didn't wake up one morning and say to themselves, "Today I'm going to cause you misery." They were both deeply anguished about my pain. They cared about me and wanted the best for me. *Your* betrayer may feel the same way.

You can still love someone who has betrayed you. But the betrayal moves you to a place of fear, which is the opposite of love. Since you feel attacked by your betrayer you want to hide first and then counterattack. You will then enrage your betrayer and create a cycle of rageful, mutually destructive attacks. As *A Course in Miracles*® tells us, being in a place of fear is not the answer. What you must ask yourself is, *"How can I get back to love again?"*

Every betrayal can be viewed as a catastrophe or as a temporary deviation from love. When you feel betrayed you have a choice: You can stay in the fear mindset or you can look at the betrayal from the perspective of love. Betrayal is an integral part of every relationship. You're receiving it now, but haven't you also done it yourself? As Dr. Warren Farrell, author of *Why Men Are the Way They Are*, wisely advises, you can either continue to attack your betrayer or start to feel compassion

---

[4.] *Radical Honesty*, New York, Dell Publishing, 1996.

for him. The first option will drive you further apart; the second will pull you closer together.[5]

When I endured my second betrayal, my husband Buddy and I managed to avoid attacking each other—most of the time. But one day he got very angry and started to stomp out the door. I placed myself in front of him and said quietly, *"You are going to leave in love."* Then I just stood there and looked into his eyes. He glared back. After what seemed like an eternity—but actually was about thirty seconds—he reached out and took my hand. I knew he had gotten my message. Betrayal can be done in fear or in love. Together we chose love.

[5] Phone interview with the author, September 13, 1996.

Chapter 4

Knowledge Is Power: Understand How the Betrayal Happened

*W*hen you discover a betrayal the first question you usually ask yourself is, "Was it my fault?" Believe it or not, the answer is, "no." Then you wonder, "What did I do to make it happen?" The truth is not nearly so much as you think.

The betrayal was beyond your control. You didn't know about it, you didn't approve of it, and you couldn't stop it. While each of us bears some responsibility for creating the circumstances that lead to a betrayal (you'll learn more about this in the next chapter), you have nothing to feel guilty about. It's the betrayer who committed the act. *He* should be feeling remorse, not you.

Betrayal Is Self-Destructive

It's a stretch to try to understand your betrayer's motivation, but you must in order to conquer your pain. Just for a moment imagine yourself playing the role of your betrayer. Feel the anxiety—or naked fear—that you're going to be exposed. You have no peace of mind because you're constantly worried that your partner is going to find out about your hidden alliance. Experience the loss of self-respect. You look in the mirror and see a person you're not proud to be. After all, you know you've destroyed your integrity. If you can't trust yourself anymore, whom can you trust? You haven't just betrayed your partner; you've betrayed yourself.

A betrayer has other painful emotions. Typically he feels:

- *Embarrassed, ashamed, and guilty.* He knows he has done something unacceptable. Self-respect diminishes as the betrayal continues.

- *Self-hating.* He despises himself for what he is doing but feels unable to stop. As time passes he may actually punish himself by getting sick or having an accident.
- *Confused.* He is torn between his loyalty to two people, both of whom mean a lot. For example, Arnold, a company vice president, is having an exciting sexual fling with his twenty-three-year-old secretary, who supports him emotionally both in and out of the office. But he still loves his wife and two teenaged sons and doesn't want to give them up.
- *Grief-stricken.* He's gaining a new relationship but at the same time he's about to lose something precious: perhaps the comfort of a long-term, trusting partnership, daily contact with his children, or the respect of fellow members of his church or synagogue.
- *Worried.* He's aware that once the betrayal is revealed he'll lose material things (income, the house, stocks, and other financial assets) and the social acceptance that goes with being half of a couple.
- *Lonely.* Although he is experiencing the joy of intimacy in his new relationship, he feels distant from his partner and uncomfortable with family members and mutual friends.
- *Helpless and overwhelmed.* Caught in a situation he doesn't know how to deal with, he knows he can't resolve it without hurting and being hurt. Not knowing how to minimize the damage he's causing, sometimes he feels like he's drowning in ten feet of water.

All of these emotions are self-destructive. People who feel ashamed, confused, grief-stricken, afraid, lonely, and helpless are at war with themselves. Your betrayer's inner turmoil may persist for years. If your relationship dissolves, he may sabotage his next one.

Betrayal Is Always Secret
Everyone has a private zone. You don't share everything about yourself even with your most intimate friends. There are some topics you'd just rather not talk about. Perhaps they're unpleasant; perhaps they're unimportant in your opinion. In either case, they're nobody's business but

your own. Maybe you'd prefer not to reveal that last month you got a traffic ticket or that you masturbated last week. You may feel comfortable sharing this information, but you'd still rather not. Everyone has boundaries and we must learn to respect them.

But if you have a secret you may feel embarrassed about what's going on. You may honestly believe that if you bring it up, you'll cause your partner to be angry or upset. You may unintentionally put him down, blame him, shame him, or, in the worst possible scenario, end your relationship. So you must keep it hidden. There may already be a thick wall of silence about other issues as well. Or you and your partner may communicate well about most subjects, but this one is an exception.

Information can be either private or secret. It depends upon who you are. For example, if you're ashamed about masturbating then it's no longer just private; it's secret. It's not an "I-can-tell-you-or-not" issue; it's an "I-better-not-tell-you-or-else" issue.

Betrayal is always secret. Why? There are many reasons. For one thing, it's a loaded issue guaranteed to cause an upset. Our cultural norm for a "happy marriage" is a sexually and emotional monogamous relationship. It's also a conflict-free relationship in which both people get along with each other smoothly and live in harmony. We are taught to avoid arguments whenever possible. We may have observed our parents handling difficult issues by sweeping them under the rug. We learned, "A good wife doesn't make waves"; "A smart husband doesn't rock the boat." Revealing a secret betrayal is guaranteed to cause a major storm.

The betrayer feels ashamed about what he has done. He's afraid of being caught, afraid of being punished, afraid of all the recriminations he will have to endure if the truth is revealed. For example, one betrayer, Andy, says, "I'm hiding out not because I enjoy it but because I feel I'm in danger. Why am I keeping my new relationship a secret? Because I might change my mind and decide to end it. Right now I'd rather my partner didn't know, so I'm willing to hide."

Again, there's no peace when you're worried that you may get caught. Over a prolonged period of time betrayers may experience physical symptoms from headaches to heart attacks. Betrayal can wreak havoc with your body.

WHY BETRAYERS DON'T TELL

There are many motivations for keeping an outside relationship secret. Which one might be your betrayer's?

- *He doesn't want to hurt you.* Every betrayer knows that sharing what he's up to will be upsetting. Initially he'd prefer to hide behind a wall of silence so you will be protected.
- *He doesn't want to face the damage.* If he possibly can, your betrayer would rather keep your family together and hold onto your jointly owned assets. After all, he doesn't want to lose what he's spent his life working for.
- *The outside relationship is so new that he isn't sure it's going to last.* Your betrayer may prefer to wait until it solidifies and he's in a stronger position.
- *His new friend is urging him not to tell* and he's succumbing to the pressure.
- *He doesn't want to be ridiculed, scolded, or humiliated.* To give it all away would be like putting himself in front of a firing squad. In the sense of a sexual betrayal, if he doesn't tell he looks good; if he does tell he looks bad.
- *He believes it's hopeless even to try.* Having experienced a profound lack of trust and acceptance in your relationship, he concludes it would only make matters worse.
- *He's waiting for you to bring up the subject.* Perhaps your betrayer has been encouraging you by hinting or leaving clues.
- *He doesn't know—or thinks he doesn't know—how to talk about it.* If he's unskilled in communicating about less important issues, how can he possibly discuss one as loaded as a betrayal?

Why is your betrayer hiding behind a wall of silence?

BETRAYERS RATIONALIZE THEIR BEHAVIOR

No one likes to feel "wrong." Your betrayer needs to justify what he has done so he can feel better about himself. Rather than facing up to the pain he's causing, he minimizes the consequences of his actions. Some typical rationalizations are:

- *I have a "good reason" for this betrayal.* My partner doesn't understand me or is "undersexed."
- *It's not hurting my partner at all.* Kevin, a construction worker who betrayed his wife a month ago, tells me, "Oh, she's doing just fine."
- *Everybody does it nowadays.* Even if the betrayer knows only a handful of other people in the same situation, he fools himself into believing his behavior is "normal."
- *I didn't do anything "wrong."* Larry, a dentist, insists, "After all, who's to say what's 'right' or 'wrong' anymore? It depends on the situation, doesn't it?"
- *I'm doing this for my family's own good.* Mel, a chef, says, "My wife wants me to be happy. So do the kids. When I feel well I treat them well. I'm a much better husband and father now that I've got another relationship. So why tell?"

By not facing the truth the betrayer avoids dealing with his guilt. This is why confrontation is so important. The betrayer must know that he is hurting you as well as your children, your extended family, and your friends.

Who Is the Accomplice?

Up to now you've been introduced to two of the main characters in the drama of betrayal: yourself and your partner. There is one more leading player whom you're ready to meet, "the accomplice."

Who is this woman to whom your partner is attracted? Someone who is willing to commit a dishonest act? Someone who is ruthlessly taking advantage of a situation and using it to her benefit? Or someone who is a flesh-and-blood human being just like you and me? The accomplice is all of these—and more.

Whoever she is, the accomplice is equally responsible for your betrayal. Someone can invite an accomplice to betray, but she doesn't have to say yes. She can always refuse to offer sexual fulfillment, emotional support, spiritual guidance, and even practical help if she believes it will threaten another person's relationship. All she has to say is, "Go find someone else." Without the accomplice's cooperation your betrayer's plot would fail.

As Chris Ketcham, who leads workshops on radical honesty, puts it, "If a married man invites me to have a sexual relationship with him and I say 'yes,' I'm facilitating his lying and cheating. I'm enabling him to betray his wife. I'm not responsible for his behavior but I'm 100 percent responsible for mine. Since I'm a person of integrity, I have an absolute duty—to him, to his spouse, and to myself—to decline. If I say "no," he may try again with someone else. I can't change that. But I myself can refuse to play his game. I can tell him, "Go back to your wife and work things out."[1]

Initially an accomplice may be innocent. But once she finds out about the plot she can choose whether or not she wants to participate in it. Nan, an administrative assistant, tells me about her friend Olivia, a belly dancer, who repeatedly asks Nan to provide an alibi. "Olivia wants me to say we're together when she's cheating on her boyfriend. She leaves messages on my answering machine telling me she's with her new lover so I know when I am supposed to be vouching for her. But I've stopped returning her calls. I don't have to play the role she is setting me up for."

Some accomplices conspire only once; others make it a habit. An experienced accomplice uses bait just like a spy. It can be sex, money, a home to relax in, a child to play with—whatever the betrayer wants most. A serial accomplice has a talent for finding out. She leaves bodies behind her just like a mass murderer. A serial accomplice doesn't actually kill anyone, but she destroys love, trust, and integrity every time she conspires. Didn't a piece of your spirit die when you found out you were betrayed?

ACCOMPLICES RATIONALIZE THEIR BEHAVIOR, TOO

Like betrayers, accomplices don't want to face what they're doing. So they comfort themselves with rationalizations such as these:

- I'm offering support to someone who's really unhappy, so I must be a good person.

---

[1] Interview with the author, April 18, 1996.

- If his wife really loved him, she would do something to get him back.
- If my friend really cared about his partner, he wouldn't be here with me. I'm innocent.
- It's better for everyone that we stay together because I'm making him so much happier than his wife can.
- Finding each other was so serendipitous that our relationship was "meant to be."
- His wife should be grateful to me because I'm taking him off her hands.

The betrayer, in turn, does his best to ensure that his accomplice doesn't feel guilty. This usually means exaggerating, distorting, or even lying. Paul, a landscaper, tells his accomplice that his wife has a boyfriend (even though she doesn't). If the accomplice sees her friend as a victim, then she may feel justified. Lee, an accountant, tells his accomplice that he and his partner haven't had sex for six months (even though they are still making love once a week). The accomplice may think, "Poor Lee, starving for sex. His partner's probably not interested anymore. Maybe she'll get jealous if she finds out about us and desire him again." In this case, the accomplice may feel that she's helping, not hurting, his other relationship.

For the accomplice to continue to rationalize she must see the betrayer's partner as an object. Words like *bitch, witch, slut,* or *tramp* may be used to describe the woman. Ideally the accomplice must never meet the partner at all. Otherwise, the accomplice may find out that the "bitch" is a shy woman with a soft voice and gentle manner or that the slut is a petite brunette who wears conservative clothing and never flirts.

UNDERSTANDING THE ACCOMPLICE

When you're betrayed, you see the accomplice as your enemy. Never did I ask myself, "Could you ever be an accomplice, Riki?" Then I was offered the opportunity—and had a chance to play the role. What a rare opportunity to see both sides: the betrayed person's and the accomplice's!

MY OWN STORY: FROM ANGER TO PERSONAL POWER

After Buddy told me about his woman friend my emotions were overwhelming. I experienced five kinds of intense feelings toward the accomplice—*anger, curiosity, sexual jealousy, insecurity,* and *empathy*—before I was able to regain my personal power.

At first I felt as if I could kill her. Although I am a gentle, peace-loving person, I had violent fantasies. I believed she was 100 percent accountable for what had happened. When Buddy approached her, she had the moral responsibility to say "no." I was furious. After I regained control, my *destructive anger* turned into healthy anger, which I shared with Buddy.

Next, my *curiosity* set in. Was she viable? Could he develop a long-term relationship with her, or was it a fly-by-night liaison? What kind of person was she? Was she prettier, sexier, or more fun to be with than I was? What did he see in her that I didn't have? It took me a while to figure out she wasn't "better," only different.

The temptation to talk to her was strong. I got hold of her phone number. All it would have taken was a few taps of my finger to make contact. Should I let her know the pain she was causing me? Fortunately, my common sense was stronger than my curiosity. I remembered the advice I always gave other people: Offer no diplomatic recognition whatsoever to an outlaw. I decided she wasn't worth a second of my time. Making even a brief connection with her would acknowledge her presence in my life. I needed to focus entirely on me. I could not afford to give her even a tiny fraction of my precious energy.

Yes, I wanted to sabotage their relationship, but I didn't. I could have told the accomplice certain facts that might have scared her away from Buddy. But I didn't want to be responsible for setting off a bomb that might destroy their relationship. If they ever broke up that would be their mutual decision. I wasn't going to have blood on my hands.

Then I had a severe case of *sexual jealousy.* Buddy and I had our problems, but we always managed to have great sex. What were he and the accomplice doing together in bed that was better? Finally I confided in a good male friend of mine who gave me this excellent advice: Stop obsessing. Don't bother yourself about the two of them; it isn't worth it. Whenever you find yourself imagining the two of them having sex, shift your thoughts to something else. Time will pass and your obsession will fade. Later on you'll have your own great sex. (He was right!)

Buddy's betrayal was devastating to my ego. He had made a powerful statement: "I prefer someone else to you." My self-esteem plummeted. I felt unloved and unlovable. If he didn't value me, how could I value me? I was desolate as I endured the agony of self-doubt. I was being tortured by *insecurity* in an emotional concentration camp.

One day I decided enough was enough. I went into my room and lay down on my bed. Breathing deeply, I created these affirmations, which I started saying to myself every morning and evening:

- *It doesn't matter whether or not Buddy loves me. I love me.*
- *My greatest gift is my own life. It is the only life I can control. I have the power to create myself exactly how I want to be.*
- *I am a beautiful person, unique and special. No one else has what I have to offer the world.*

Now I was focusing on myself instead of on the accomplice. Gradually I noticed my attitude changing. The energy I had been using to obsess about the accomplice's attractive qualities was now being directed inward. Instead of continually asking myself, "What's so special about her?" I was asking, "What's special about me?" My personal power was being reborn.

My vision was further expanded after a conversation with Eileen Broer, a personal growth seminar leader and a good friend of mine. She assured me that after the dust had settled I would want to send the accomplice a dozen roses instead of arsenic. Why? Because the accomplice was a catalyst in my personal growth. The betrayal was an invitation to look at my life, to assess what was wrong with it, and to move ahead to fulfill my own dreams.[2] At first Eileen's statements sounded preposterous to me, but they soon became my guideposts.

Then a "miracle" happened. While I was attending a professional convention I was introduced to a married man from out of town. We were immediately attracted to each other. I was starving for sex and affection and he was offering me both. How I wanted him!

[2.] Phone conversation with the author, June 3, 1996.

Here was a revelation. I myself was now being tempted to play the role of accomplice, the very one I'd been condemning. I found myself rationalizing: "Never mind that he's married; after all, he's told me he is unhappy with his wife and is getting ready to leave her." I felt the accomplice's intense passion, the temptation, the motivation to throw caution to the winds. In short, I wanted to do exactly what Buddy's woman friend had done.

During the next six months we kept in touch by phone. I searched my soul. Could I ever become an accomplice? I thought of how a sexual liaison between us might affect his wife and two children, three innocent people completely unaware of what was going on. The only way we could in good conscience have a romantic relationship was if his wife knew. "Tell her you've met someone you're attracted to," I kept urging him. "No," he repeatedly replied. We were at an impasse. Eventually the two of us realized how hurtful a secret connection could be. We decided not to have an affair; he stayed with his wife; and I returned to my own path of personal growth, much wiser and more humble.

How a Betrayal Unfolds

Betrayal is a drama in three acts. *You* are the star of the show. Each act has two scenes, with a main theme:

> Act I: The Initial Shock
> > Scene 1: Denying It: "This Can't Be Happening to Me."
> > Scene 2: Grappling with Guilt: "It's All My Fault."
> Act II: The Facts Emerge
> > Scene 1: Confronting the Betrayer: "How Could You Do This to Me?"
> > Scene 2: Listening to the Confession: "Can I Ever Forgive You?"
> Act III: Betrayal is a Wake-Up Call
> > Scene 1: Dealing with the Fallout: "What Shall I Do Next?"
> > Scene 2: Rebuilding My Life: "I Have the Power to Create Myself Exactly How I Want to Be."

We will discuss scenes from the first two acts next.

DENYING IT

"Denial." It ain't just a river in Egypt, as almost every psychotherapist knows. Denial is real—and it can be healthy. By refusing to believe something awful has happened you protect yourself from pain until you are ready to feel it. A major betrayal is not only agonizing but also incredible. It's a shock to find out that your precious trust has been violated. When you say, "This can't be happening to me," you are sincere.

Quincy, a registered nurse who was married for twelve years, sobs: "Everything seemed just fine. Richard was a model husband. He gave me presents on my birthday, flowers for our anniversary, and hugs and kisses in between. He'd even go grocery shopping and bring me breakfast in bed on Sunday mornings. Our sex life was exciting, at least for me. So when he told me he had been secretly dating someone else for more than a year, my reaction was, 'Say what?'" Sarah, a lawyer married to a paralegal, explains, "I'm in shock. We've both been so busy with two jobs, three kids, volunteer work, and our house in the mountains that I can't possibly figure out how Tom had the time to betray me." Elizabeth, who was married for twenty years, notes, "I had refused to believe that there was anything seriously wrong in my marriage. I traveled a lot on business, but so do lots of women. My husband never told me he was in love with my best friend. I refused to look at what was going on. Why? Because I had a lot at stake. First of all, I still loved my husband. Second, I didn't want to lose his financial support. Third, and most important, I was afraid of losing full access to my kids."

WATCH OUT FOR BLACK FLAGS

Elizabeth's story is not untypical. You sense a betrayal on an unconscious level long before you become consciously aware of it. Almost always there are signs (I call them "black flags") that indicate there's something wrong:

- *Your partner's sexual behavior changes.* He doesn't want sex as often; he wants it more often; or he introduces new sexual techniques he's never learned from you.
- *Your partner's emotional pattern changes.* He starts getting angry at you for no good reason; he becomes distant and some-

times doesn't even hear what you are saying; or suddenly he
becomes incredibly sweet and ingratiating.
- *Your partner's physical habits change.* He starts working out
regularly at the gym; he spends much more time taking especially good care of his body; or he goes on a healthy, or not-so-
healthy food binge.
- *Your partner's lifestyle changes.* He begins to have regular
unexplained absences from home; he routinely works late at
the office (when he's rarely done this before); or he frequently leaves the house on the pretext of "doing an errand."

Yes, you should have noticed that something was going on. A sexually, emotionally, or physically absent partner is likely to be getting fulfillment somewhere else. Your partner was giving you messages that you
didn't want to hear. Once or twice you may have asked a question but
then backed off. It's easy to do; we all prefer to believe what we want
to believe.

According to Dr. Brad Blanton, Gestalt psychologist and author of
Radical Honesty, "As soon as you ask your very first question you are
admitting to yourself that you are suspicious. If your partner gives you
a vague answer about what's going on you have a choice: you can allow
it to happen or you can resist it. Either you can accept his refusal to give
you the information you requested, or you can say, 'If you won't answer
my question, if you won't talk to me, if you won't give the details of
what's happening to you, I'm out of here.'"

I myself asked my first question when Buddy's woman friend called
our house at 11:00 P.M. on his birthday. "Who is she?" I inquired. "Oh,
someone I met when I was out of town. I rented a room in her house
for a while," he responded. I didn't press him further. Was it a mistake?
Yes and no. No, because I was completely unprepared to deal with the
betrayal. Yes, because deep inside I knew something was going on. From
that moment on I shifted into "let's pretend" gear: acting like everything
was fine instead of admitting that something serious was wrong. I was
in denial. Buddy and I pretended everything was fine for five months
before I was ready to face the truth.

Getting past denial is hell. A thousand thoughts rush through your mind. "The incredible has happened. The world has turned upside down. The unbelievable is believable. The impossible is possible. Everything I've believed was true is false. The person I thought I could count on most has betrayed me." According to Dr. Judith Sherven and Dr. James Sniechowski, relationship seminar coleaders and coauthors of *The New Intimacy*,[3] it's not just the loss of a love, it's the end of innocence." Never again will you completely believe in anything or anyone.

GRAPPLING WITH GUILT

When denial finally passes and you get a grip on reality, your first thoughts are, "It's all my fault. I should have known what was going on. I ought to have done something to prevent this."

None of these statements are true. While you did play a role in what happened, your partner and his accomplice both made a deliberate choice to betray you. They were aware of what they were doing. In all likelihood there was absolutely nothing you could have done. Yes, at first you feel at fault, but you must overcome your guilt. If you allow it to persist you will punish yourself. Instead, you need to begin to heal.

Betrayal is a fact of life. There's nothing to feel guilty about or ashamed of. Stand up and declare that you've been betrayed, and many of your friends will tell you, "It's happened to me, too." If you're even more courageous, form a betrayal support group. Reach out to people you've never met before. Volunteer your living room once a month, place a classified ad in your local newspaper, and see who shows up. You'll find out that you are not alone. A nationwide network of these groups needs to be formed, and I offer you my sincere encouragement. We must start sharing our stories and validating each other's experiences en masse.

CONFRONTING THE BETRAYER

GETTING READY

Confronting a betrayal is overwhelming at first. Your mouth gets dry, your hands start to shake, and you break out in a cold sweat every

---

3. *The New Intimacy*, Deerfield Beach, Florida, Health Communications Inc., 1997.

time you think of bringing up the subject. Why? Ask yourself, "What am I afraid of?"

- *My partner may not want to have sex with me anymore.*
- *My partner may deny what I'm saying.*
- *My partner may make fun of me or put me down.*
- *My partner may reject me or leave me.*
- *My partner may become violent.*

These are all real fears. Identify which ones are uppermost for you. Then deal with them one at a time:

- *My partner may not want to have sex with me anymore.* You're better off not having sex with your partner. The two of you are probably going through the motions anyway, and if he's sleeping with someone else you may be putting your life at risk.
- *My partner may deny what I'm saying.* Yes, your partner may flatly contradict you. Be prepared to stand your ground. If you turn out to be wrong, that's good news. You can always apologize later. If you're right, the truth will set you both free.
- *My partner may make fun of me or put me down.* Isn't this less painful than living a lie?
- *My partner may reject me or leave me.* Your partner has, in fact, already rejected you. He may also leave you eventually whether or not you confront him. If he's on the way out, confronting the betrayal will strengthen you in the long run. If he stays, at least you will have initiated an honest conversation.
- *My partner may become violent.* This is a real fear and it needs to be addressed. For your personal safety you must convince a friend to be with you during the confrontation. If your friend can't be present, then agree that you can use your friend's house as a refuge in an emergency. It's important to know that if you have to leave your house you'll have a place to go. At the very least, ask your friend to be near the phone so if your emotions get out of control you can leave the room and call.

Take time to prepare yourself for the confrontation scene. Yes, you're red hot with rage. You have a right to be angry. But an attack-defend session (you attack, he defends, and then vice versa) isn't going to help either of you an ounce, except to allow you to let off steam. If you say cruel, hurtful things to each other you may create lasting enmity, which is definitely not in your best interest. Your intention is to rebuild your life, not to destroy it.

Before you confront your betrayer express your rage—safely. You can let off steam by yourself, with a good friend, in a support group setting, or in a psychotherapist's office—wherever is most comfortable. Close the windows and scream. Punch a pillow or use a red foam bat[4] to hit your bed. Clean your house from top to bottom. Go for a long jog (run until you feel exhausted), play a couple of sets of tennis (doesn't it feel wonderful to slam that ball?), or have a friendly wrestling match with a good friend (agree that she or he won't let you get out of control). Or write a letter to your betrayer (but don't send it). You may also want to compose a song, write a poem, create a painting, or make a collage. Whichever method you choose, be sure to let out your feelings of fury, despair, and even hope:

- How could you be so untrue after everything I've done for you?
- You liar. I'll never believe another word you say again.
- You have incinerated my life. But I will rise from the ashes.
- Right now I hate you. Someday I will thank you for setting me free, for giving me the chance to become a better me.

Each time you vent your emotions, you must perform a healing ritual afterward. Remember, blowing your top sends tension all through your body; it's a fight or flight response to the threat of betrayal. You have to release the tension in order to feel centered. Light a candle, burn some incense, put on your favorite tape or compact disk, or lie down, and breathe deeply for at least three minutes. Or create your own unique healing ritual. Your goal is to relax and regain your strength.

[4.] Psychotherapist Martha Baldwin Beveridge can sell you one of these red foam bats. Write to her at Options Now, Inc., 901 N.W. 62nd Street, Oklahoma City, Oklahoma 73118.

YOU ARE THE STAR OF THE SHOW

A time will come when you're ready to face what's happening. In the case of betrayal, knowledge is power. The confrontation is a critical step in your healing. Once the betrayer's secret is out he no longer has the upper hand. You are on equal footing again.

Why is confrontation so important? Because your mental and physical health is at stake. Remaining silent allies you with your betrayer; you, he, and the accomplice are all conspiring to keep the secret intact. The stress can affect your body. You may wind up in your dentist's office if you grind your teeth, run up thousands of dollars in doctor's bills if you get high blood pressure, or find yourself commuting to your chiropractor's if you injure your back. The stress can also affect your mind. You may be called into your boss's office for being distracted at work, get a traffic ticket for careless driving, or even wind up at the police station for being involved in a traffic accident. These woes are all painful— and avoidable.

How do you stage a confrontation? *On your terms.* Remember, you're directing this play as well as acting in it. *You* pick the time and place. *You* decide what you're going to say. *You* end the conversation whenever you're ready.

Remember, your purpose is to find out the information you need so you can decide how best to proceed. So instead of starting a fight, play the role of detective. Imagine that the betrayal is a mystery and your job is to solve it. Before you can make judgments you have to know what's going on.

Pretend you're a journalist covering a story. All reporters know that before they sit down to write an article they need to get as many facts as possible. When asking questions, they use the "five Ws": who, what when, where, and why.

- *Who* is involved?
- *What* exactly is happening?
- *When* did it begin?
- *Where* does it take place?
- *Why* has it occurred?

Your partner's answers may as brief as these:

- Me and Susie.
- We're having sex every weekend.
- Last year.
- In a motel.
- Because our sex life is lousy.

Or your discussion may go on well into the night and continue in daily installments as ours did.

If you're comfortable, bring a notebook and pen with you and take notes just as a reporter would. It will give you something to do with your hands while your partner is talking, encourage him to take your questions more seriously, and enable you to have a record of what he actually said. If your partner refuses to reply, make it clear that his silence is unacceptable to you. You have a right to know what is going on. You are going to persist until you get some answers.

No matter how difficult the confrontation becomes, keep in mind that it is your pathway to health. You are not only giving yourself an opportunity to understand what's going on but also making your partner witness your pain—and paving the way for his making amends to you. After all, your betrayer is not supposed to walk away from the damage scot-free. You have a responsibility to show him the consequences of his actions. Speak your mind. You are powerful in your righteous indignation. Let your partner know the pain and anguish you are experiencing: "How could you hurt me this way?" Perhaps he'll think twice before betraying again.

If you have evidence of the betrayal now is the time to show it. And I don't just mean a lipstick-stained shirt. After Buddy confronted me I took out all the symbols of our commitment to each other including our marriage certificate, our wedding invitation, my long white dress, the beautiful combs I had worn in my hair, the pressed dried flower he had worn in his lapel, and all the thoughtful cards we had received from friends and put them on display in our bedroom. After six weeks he asked me to put them away. I complied because I had already made my point. For forty-two days he had viewed tangible reminders of the broken promise.

Showing off the evidence is important. A decade earlier, when a boyfriend of mine broke our relationship off without explanation and wouldn't return my phone calls, I waited outside his apartment until he let me in. I told him exactly how I felt—and I also asked him for the two glass casserole dishes and other pots and pans I had left behind. While they weren't as powerful as a wedding dress or a marriage certificate, they did symbolize his betrayal. My props enhanced the drama.

WHAT TO DO IF YOUR BETRAYER CONFRONTS YOU

What if your partner confronts you with his betrayal? This happens occasionally. Study these guidelines so you can act instead of react. Prepare yourself to guide the conversation. Although Buddy actually initiated our confrontation, the scenario was the same as if I had brought up the subject.

OVERCOMING YOUR RESISTANCE TO CONFRONTATION

It's possible that your betrayer has actually tried to tell you about what's going on but you inadvertently thwarted him. Maybe the conversation never even got started. You may have said, "Yes, I know you have something you want to discuss but I'm busy right now with the kids," "I'm on my way out to a meeting," or "I'm so tired—can't it wait till the morning?" After a few attempts your betrayer may have given up. Or you may have stopped the conversation after it started. If you're still in denial, you may drop the subject and leave the room stating, "I don't want to talk about it."

You may also receive the message with disbelief: "I simply don't understand what you're saying to me." You may even misunderstand it: "Yes I'm aware that occasionally you have dinner with Abby but we've already agreed that's all it's going to amount to." Or, if you're almost ready to face the truth, you may interrupt or contradict your partner so many times that he never gets to tell his story at all. It's a rare betrayer who will persist in sharing what's going on when his partner isn't open to hearing about it.

Ask yourself, "Could my partner be trying to tell me the truth?" If you've been resisting, don't blame yourself. Sometimes it's a good idea to wait a while before a confrontation. You need to build up your inner confidence, get past denial, and look for a persistent pattern of black flags so that you don't ruin a good relationship with false accusations. Finally, you have to learn how to stage a confrontation.

WHEN CONFRONTATION IS IMPOSSIBLE

What if you can't confront? I've had this happen myself. Charles chose not to admit his betrayal directly to me. But I wasn't going to let him keep me from processing my emotions. Instead, I shared my story with everyone who was willing to listen: my friends; my family; and, when I could afford it, a psychotherapist. I also talked openly to my children; after all, Charles had betrayed all of us. (I'll discuss how to communicate with kids in Chapter 7.) In particular, sharing my betrayal with others who had had a common experience was incredibly healing. I realized that I wasn't alone; lots of people I knew had also been betrayed. A few told me stories that were actually more horrendous than mine.

Sometimes a supportive, qualified third party can facilitate a confrontation. A friend of mine, who was going to a psychotherapist, was betrayed by her partner. When he wouldn't discuss the betrayal she gave him an open invitation to join her in the therapist's office. So far he hasn't shown up, but the door is still open.

LISTENING TO YOUR BETRAYER'S CONFESSION

Your betrayer's confession may take only a few minutes or it may take several hours. He may refuse to answer you the first time you confront him but he may open up at a later moment when you least expect it. After all, your partner's caught in a dilemma. He'll hurt you by telling the truth but he'll injure you even more in the long run by continuing to lie. As one man put it, "Why should I tell my wife if I'm going to destroy all the beautiful trust we've built up over the years? On the other hand, she's going to find out eventually and then it's really going to 'hit the fan,'"

It's not easy to decide to confess. Abe, a graduate student in English, told me, "It was very difficult for me to tell Billy, the pal I'd been staying with for almost three months, that his girlfriend and I were secretly in love. He was going to Europe for a while and it would have been easy to avoid the issue. But I realized that if he were to find out from someone else without hearing from me first he'd feel terrible. And how would I feel in the future sneaking around—always knowing that my good friend didn't know the truth? I just couldn't live with myself."

He continued, "I knew I needed some support to get the courage to confess, so I told another good friend about my dilemma. He understood and offered to help. Together we talked to Billy and got everything out in the open. Will our friendship survive the crisis? Will we be as good friends as we were before? I don't know. Only time will tell. But I do know that by being honest with him I feel better about myself. I can look in the mirror, stare into my eyes, and say to myself, 'I have integrity.'"

When *your* betrayer takes the plunge, bite your tongue and listen with your heart. If your feelings get too painful or intense, excuse yourself. Return only when you've cooled off. If you feel you're about to lose control, call a friend while you're out of the room and ask your friend to stand by. Do your best not to interrupt, criticize, or judge. Maintain a bit of detachment if you possibly can; try pretending that your partner is someone else telling a story about three people you've never met. By playing it smart you'll most likely get the facts you need even if it takes several "confession sessions."

Chapter 5

Why Did He Do It?

*W*hen you are betrayed you don't understand why. You feel confused. You feel overwhelmed. You feel powerless. But you *can* turn the tide. Although passion and desperation are the most common reasons for choosing to betray, everyone's motivation is different. Understanding the unique origins of your own betrayal enables you to deal with it more effectively and regain your strength more quickly.

Possible Origins of the Betrayal

AN ACT OF PASSION

Believe it or not, betrayers aren't monsters. They are decent human beings, many with deep integrity, who are driven by intense desire. Many love their partner and don't want to hurt her. But if their flames of passion are fanned high enough, they lose sight of the consequences of their actions. All of us have the potential to betray.

A CONSCIOUS CHOICE

Betrayal is usually a conscious choice. The betrayer asks himself two questions: "How deeply am I attracted to the other person? Could I possibly forget her?" The betrayer weighs the answers and makes a decision. Rarely does he go on to inquire, "How will I damage my existing relationship? What are the long-term consequences of my actions? Is it worth it?" Short-term gain overrides long-term pain.

A person who betrays feels exhilarated at first. But his euphoria soon turns to misery. Why? Just for a minute, imagine yourself as a betrayer. You love your partner, but feel she doesn't love you. You are out on a date or lying next to your spouse in bed, and you feel totally alone. You are reaching out with warmth and affection but not getting anything back. That's how some betrayers feel day after day.

Continue your effort to get inside a typical betrayer's head. You would also feel unappreciated. For example, Chad, a taxi driver, says "I bring her flowers, I take her to concerts, I do the laundry, I take the kids to the park—and she takes it all for granted. When I mention how I'd like more attention and appreciation, she mutters, 'Men are insatiable.'" Dorothy, an administrative assistant, echoes this sentiment. "When I come home after a hard day at work, the dog is more excited to see me than he is. All I get is a routine peck on the cheek and then he goes about his business. I've told him how I feel, but he doesn't seem to care."

Typically a betrayer believes he has sincerely tried to get through to his partner, but to no avail. His first choice would be to save the relationship, but if he can't, then he'll turn to someone else. Betrayal is often a deed that comes as a last resort.

A FEELING OF DESPERATION

Most of us are uncomfortable in our relationships now and then. From time to time we feel like chucking it and checking out. But we don't. We realize that commitment means being there for the downs as well as the ups. In order to keep what you have—partner, home, and children—you have to give something up. Your betrayer wants it all. He's not ready to make a final decision to exit, but he doesn't want to walk away from emotional or sexual ecstasy. If your betrayer could express what is in his heart he would say, "What I'm feeling is so important to me that I'm willing to sacrifice my integrity, my self-respect, the moral standards I was raised with, and even my physical and mental health in order to hold onto it."

Betrayal is rooted in desperation. We betray someone only when our feelings are so intense that we simply can't ignore them.

UNMET NEEDS AND UNEXPRESSED FEELINGS

Your betrayer is a lonely, frustrated person trying to get his needs met. He has intense, unexpressed feelings that he seeks to share. Here's a list of the fourteen most common needs and feelings.

1. *Sexual frustration* is what propels many betrayers. Eric, a television producer, is placing personal ads in a local newspaper that don't mention that he's married. Why? He says, "I'm finding some women to date. My marriage isn't all that good. As a matter of fact, we're in counseling right now. But it doesn't solve my problem. My wife and I haven't made love for six months and that's something I can't ignore." Other betrayers are having sex but they are afraid to ask their partner to fulfill their deepest erotic desires: phone sex, cybersex, swinging sex, or some other kind of sex they'd like to experience. Some betrayers are just not physically attracted to their spouse anymore. Perhaps she's gained twenty pounds, gotten twenty years older, or can't carry on a sexually titillating conversation for twenty minutes. A betrayer is someone who is yearning to be turned on.

2. *Resentment* is another prevalent feeling. The betrayer must ventilate his stored-up anger. The betrayal may be a way of getting even. Frank, a clerk at a grocery shop, is having a sexual relationship with the woman across the street. Every day after work, he stops off at home, has a cocktail, and then goes over to her house. He tells her that he hasn't been getting enough attention from his spouse, and they have sex. Frank knows exactly where he is and what he is doing. He is deliberately hurting her partner.

3. A betrayer seeks *intimacy*. He craves someone to feel close with, who can literally "see into me." Guy, a government employee, feels emotionally distant from his wife. She's so busy with the children that they have no private time together anymore. But he can confide in his secretary. The two of them have opened their hearts, souls, and minds to each other and no one, including his wife, can tear them apart.

4. An important and often overlooked cause of betrayal is *spiritual emptiness*. A couple may lack a common connection with the divine that gives meaning to their lives—and to their relationship. When someone comes along who fills the betrayer's spiritual void, her energy is like a magnet with steel.

5. The person who feels the least *power* usually betrays a relationship. One way to feel more powerful is to begin a new relationship. Secretly, it's two against one.
6. Your betrayer may believe he is *entitled* to a kind of happiness he doesn't find in your relationship. He may be thinking, "Is this all I'm going to get from our relationship? It's not enough—or it's not what I want. I deserve more—or something different."
7. Your betrayer may have felt *trapped*. "I needed freedom," is a common explanation betrayers give. Could this be true in your situation? The responsibilities of a monogamous relationship or an expensive lifestyle may have been too heavy for him. There was no way he could have known beforehand; he didn't feel the burden until after he made the commitment.
8. *Love* is what all of us seek, including betrayers. Harriet, a physician, believes her husband only values her for what she does: earn money, provide household services, and look good when they go out. She explains, "In my marriage I feel like an object. If I stopped performing, my husband wouldn't love me anymore. Isaac, my lover, accepts me exactly as I am: sometimes lazy, sometimes crazy, and sometimes with messy hair. If I were fired from my job, got sick, or lost my good looks, he'd still care about me. When we're together I feel cherished and special."
9. Behind every betrayal is usually a *hurt ego*. Joe, a banker, believes he isn't getting the attention and appreciation he deserves. He's met Karina—who's telling him how youthful he is, how sexy he is, and what a wonderful person he is. "Sometimes it sounds like flattery but I don't care." Joe says. "It sure feels good to me."
10. Like everyone else, your betrayer has *unfulfilled fantasies*. He may dream about a partner half his age—one with "movie star" looks or one with enough money for travel and other luxuries. While most people understand that their fantasies are imaginary, a betrayer actually tries to realize them.
11. *Unacknowledged changes* lead to betrayals. As time passes, each of us evolves into a different person. The gap between a couple can widen when one person experiences a major change and it

is not openly discussed. He may seek an alliance with a third person who is on the same "wave length" as he is right now.

12. Your partner may have recently gotten in touch with deep inner yearnings that he himself may not have known about. If these *hidden truths* are not revealed to you, a betrayal may be imminent. Brand-new sexual desires are the most difficult to come to terms with—and to share.

13. If your partner is *addicted to alcohol or drugs,* betrayal is an accident waiting to happen. A substance addict bonds quickly with someone else who shares his habit. If you decide to insist that your partner quit (and for good reason!), he may connect with someone more sympathetic behind your back.

14. *Yearning to be (or not to be) a parent* is another feeling many betrayers have. Some want to be free of their enormous family responsibilities; others who have had no biological children with their partner want a baby of their own. Buddy, who never had experienced fatherhood, left me for a woman who had a ready-made young child.

Which of these fourteen kinds of needs and emotions might your betrayer have? Could he be feeling sexually frustrated, resentful, lonely, spiritually empty, powerless, entitled to more than he is getting, trapped, unloved, unappreciated, misunderstood, or unhappy with his children (or lack of them)?

Nature abhors a vacuum. When a betrayer experiences a lot of dissatisfaction or distance in his relationship, there is room for someone else to fill the void. If your partner has intense feelings he can't express to you, he may turn to someone else. That's how a betrayal begins. Len's wife has been grieving about the death of her father in an automobile accident. At first she shared her sadness; now she's retreated into cold silence. Two months ago Len met Melody, a ballet dancer. He notes, "For the first time in two years I'm experiencing real joy. I feel truly alive, in and out of bed. No matter what, I must hold on to this feeling. I can't let it go."

As this energy intensifies, the betrayer wants to spend more time with the third person. A deep attachment develops. Nathan, a minister, describes how his betrayal evolved: "Finally I met Patricia. She listens to my complaints about my spouse, takes my side, and empathizes with my pain. She reassures me that I've done everything I can to make my marriage work (which I know I have). I can count on her for good fun and great sex. And she makes a big fuss over me instead of taking me for granted." Eventually the betrayer abandons his loyalty to his partner and gives it to the other person. It took eighteen months for Nathan to tell Patricia, "You are my true friend. My partner isn't. You really love me. My partner doesn't. You fulfill my sexual fantasies. My partner won't. So now you come first."

BETRAYAL IS ABOUT SEXUAL FRUSTRATION

Sex is like money: The more you lack it, the more you crave it. Whenever I appear on a radio talk show the first question I am usually asked is, "What can I do if I want sex more often than my partner does?" If you prefer to have sex once a month and your partner desires it once a day, and the two of you don't reach a mutually satisfactory agreement, you are inviting betrayal.

Life's greatest pleasure is sex. But even sex can become as routine as brushing your teeth. Same time, same place, same clothing (or lack of it), same foreplay (or lack of foreplay), same position, same mumbled words afterward. You can practically predict the scenario. What about variety, adventure, and fantasy, the ingredients of a fulfilling sex life? Having the same kind of sex day after day drives many people into a frenzy, which often ends up as a betrayal.

Men often tell me that sexual boredom is the number one reason they betray. Ralph, a librarian, confides, "I invited her to watch an X-rated movie, wear some sensuous clothing, join me at the computer to visit an erotic Web site, or have phone sex when I am in the office or out of town, but she refuses. After a while, I gave up. If she won't give me the sexual variety I need to feel alive, then I have to find another outlet. So I started visiting computer Web sites and downloading photos—alone. I fantasize about the women I see and imagine I am having sex with the most attractive one. One night on the phone, a friend of mine started telling me about her fantasies. She must have sensed that my sexual energy is exploding. Then she asked me out to dinner and I accepted. What's a guy to do? My body's on fire. We ended up having sex afterward, and it was really exciting. Of course I want to see her again."

A betrayer makes the choice either to remain sexually exclusive or to go outside of the relationship. Deep within he knows, "If I have hot sex with someone else I may not be able to keep up the old routine. Our sex will become less frequent. I may end up withdrawing all my sexual energy from you and giving it to a new partner. You may start having sex with someone else. If you find out what's going on we'll have a crisis. We may even break up. Is it worth it?"

Might your betrayer have been sexually frustrated?

BETRAYAL IS ABOUT RESENTMENT

Your betrayer has a volcano of hidden anger within. Rather than expressing his anger directly to you in a healthy way, he smothered his feelings and pretended everything was fine. But repressed anger doesn't die. Instead it smoldered, became resentment, and showed up as a betrayal.

For example, let's say your betrayer is furious at you because you never are on time for dates. He feels unimportant and unloved, as if your time together doesn't matter to you. Your betrayer can express his feelings to you directly and make a specific request, "From now on we'll agree on a time you'll be ready. If you're more than fifteen minutes late, I'll go out by myself." If you agree, then you're both dealing with the source of the anger and taking action to stop what's causing it.

But if your betrayer swallows his rage weekend after weekend, then a red-hot burn will fester. He may start being late for your dates, too. Or else he may lose your digital clock or forget your birthday, whichever will annoy you the most. Another way to get back at you is to begin a secret relationship with someone who does show up on time and gives your betrayer much-needed attention and appreciation as well. As long as you don't find out, your betrayer can express his rage indirectly and get his needs met at the same time. It's a Band-Aid—and it's secret revenge.

Could your betrayer have felt resentment toward you about something but couldn't express it directly?

BETRAYAL IS ABOUT LACK OF INTIMACY

Other betrayers feel emotionally distant from their partner. Steve, a hardware store manager, says, "Yes, we share a home, a joint checking account, and a bed. But it's like we're sailboats in the night. We pass by each other; we glance at each other, but we don't really connect. In spite of everything we have in common, we're leading separate lives, perhaps going in two different directions. She's all wrapped up in the children, and I'm totally involved in my work and my own personal growth. Our conversations are two monologues: She's telling me how our son took his first step today, and I'm telling her about how I'm starting another screenplay and looking for a new psychotherapist. Both of us are talking and neither of us is listening. There's no real intimacy. We're just discussing business; we're not sharing what we're really feeling inside."

As Dr. Warren Farrell, author of *Why Men Are the Way They Are* puts it, "No one ever gets a divorce who says, 'My partner understands me.'"[1] It's a small step from emotional disconnection to a sexual freeze. When you don't feel "heard," you don't feel sexually desirable or sexual desire for your partner. You are starving for intimacy so you open up to someone else. Then you're ready to betray.

Could there have been a deep emotional gulf between the two of you that drove your partner away?

BETRAYAL IS ABOUT SEPARATION FROM SPIRIT

Many of us go through the daily motions of living but find no real meaning in what we do. We're playing the "human game," as we endlessly seek more money and more power but find no real satisfaction. We worry about what the future holds: Could we be the next victims of a carjacking, robbery, or even murder? We feel isolated, lonely, and separated from spirit.

Without a spiritual dimension life can become a series of empty, lonely routines. Fear may prevail, instead of love. One member of a couple may feel overwhelmed by duties, such as caring for an aging parent or a sick child, or feel stuck in a boring, routine job. The other may be depressed over the recent death of a loved one. The intangible link that can unite them throughout all their ups and downs may be weak or missing entirely.

Many of us need a connection with a higher power, greater intelligence, God—call it what you will—to make sense of our human condition. Couples who worship together by meditating at home or going to

[1] *Why Men Are the Way They Are*, New York, McGraw-Hill, 1986.

church or synagogue can create a spiritual tie that binds them together in a common search for meaning.

When a couple lacks this spiritual bond, one person or the other may sometimes feel driven to go outside the relationship to find it. Your betrayer may be attending a different place of worship, going to a meditation center, or becoming part of a new religious community. When a friend is found who understands this spiritual emptiness and who can help answer the questions he's asking, an incredibly powerful emotional bond can be formed. The two friends may learn to communicate with each other in their own special language. Tom, a masseuse, tells me, "My lover and I say things to each other like "a divine energy has brought us together. We're soulmates. Our spirits are in complete harmony. This is what I've been searching for all my life." Unable to talk to his spouse about what was happening, he betrayed.

Might your betrayer have felt a spiritual emptiness in your relationship and sought fulfillment with someone else?

BETRAYAL IS ABOUT POWERLESSNESS

Your betrayer may have felt powerless in your relationship. Rightly or wrongly, he believed that you usually got your needs met and he didn't. Whenever the two of you disagreed he didn't negotiate; he let you have your way. He'd say, "Whatever you want, dear," even when the issue was really important. Or "Never mind, it's okay," when it wasn't okay with him at all. He may have felt he never got his way. If you repeatedly hear phrases such as these, chances are there is a power imbalance.

Normally, power in a relationship is dynamic; it shifts from one person to another like a seesaw.[2] But sometimes one person has all the power and becomes bossy and controlling. The other person feels as if he's under his partner's thumb. So he rebels. One of the most likely forms of rebellion is betrayal.

Once your betrayer starts another relationship behind your back he feels in charge. He says things to himself like:

- I'm doing something secret and you can't stop me.

[2.] See Chapter 6 of my book *Negotiating Love*, New York, Ballantine, 1995.

- You can make me do what you want when we're together, but I have another special relationship where I can do exactly what I want.
- You may be my boss, but there's someone else whom I boss around.
- It's two against one; I've got leverage of my own now.
- I know something you don't; I've got a secret source of strength.

The betrayal is a soothing outlet. The betrayer thinks, "I don't have to feel bad anymore," or "I know what I'm doing would hurt you if you found out, so I'm not alone in my pain." And the betrayal is also a fallback position: "If I leave you or you leave me, I'll have someone else waiting in the wings."

As long as you don't know what's going on, you become a supporting actress in a play that your partner is directing. While you've been looking the other way he's unilaterally orchestrated a whole new scene. It's a macabre plot designed to facilitate your partner's escape from your relationship. Instead of being in center stage, you're hanging out in the wings and playing a role you don't enjoy. The truth is you don't know what will happen next. To regain your power, you must find out.

Could your betrayer have felt helpless in your relationship and betrayed you to regain his power?

BETRAYAL IS ABOUT ENTITLEMENT

"I have the right to be happy" is a new personal ethic that was born in the sixties. Unlike our grandparents and parents, who probably put their obligations ahead of their personal happiness, we now give self-fulfillment a high priority. Your betrayer probably knows at least a few other people who sneaked outside their relationship to find what they were missing. "Why not me?" he may have asked himself. "Two of my friends have done it." The social pressure to say "no, I'll suffer in silence" simply isn't there anymore.

Ironically, people with a strong sense of their own personal value are the most likely to betray. Your betrayer may have been unhappy; if he believed he deserved something better, he had reason to go outside of your relationship to find it. If, on the other hand, he had thought,

"I'm not worth much," likely he would not have betrayed you. A person with low self-esteem will stay where he is and be miserable because he doesn't feel entitled to get his needs met anywhere else.

But even people with low self-esteem will betray if they're desperate enough. "I'm not acting like a spoiled child," Vince, who is in therapy, tells me. "I just have to have a shred of happiness while I'm alive. Right now I have none. I don't want to have it all; I just want to be with my lover."

Could your betrayer feel entitled to something vital he's not getting from you?

BETRAYAL IS ABOUT FEELING TRAPPED

Many betrayers feel like caged lions. There are experiences they long to have, fantasies they yearn to realize, goals they ache to pursue. Your betrayer may desperately want to be free. A betrayal may have offered him the opportunity to escape. He may have perceived your relationship as a suffocating straightjacket, not as a cradle of opportunity for the fulfillment of his dreams.

Freedom means different things to different people. Some crave the freedom to move in a different direction; others want to pursue a new career or retire, a lifestyle that their partner will not accept. Alonzo, who speaks fluent Spanish, dreams of moving to Latin America, but his wife won't hear of it. One night he meets an Argentine woman and starts dating her secretly. Beth has decided to become a minister but her husband scoffs at her plan. She starts attending classes at a local church and falls in love with her teacher. They begin spending every spare minute together without her husband's knowledge. Both Alonzo and Beth have betrayed their spouses because they need a partner who will support them in their quest.

Your betrayer may find his lifestyle suffocating. Perhaps you have children and he feels overwhelmed by their demands. Both of you honestly believed you wanted kids, but now life has become an endless round of late-night crying instead of late-night sex. If you want to go out for the evening you have to hire a babysitter. It's too much trouble. Your romance is in intensive care.

Social and economic pressures drive many people to betray. For men, the message is, "Work harder, make more money. The kids need shoes; I need a trip to Cancun." Women hear, "Keep the house clean, look attractive all the time, drive in the carpool, and be ready for sex every night." Candy is about to betray her husband. She says, "There's no space in our relationship just to hang out and be me. There's no time to just hang out and relax. There's no one to confide in about my worries: that I just got turned down for a raise and my sex drive is at an all-time low. While I pretend to be perfect, tension is building up inside me. My new friend provides what's missing. For a few hours a week I feel accepted exactly for how I am. I'm not being evaluated; I'm being loved."

Many men tell me that they feel sexually trapped. They want to date more than one person but their girlfriends have said, "Absolutely not." Some of these men want friendship, but most desire new sexual experiences. A media personality called me up to ask me to have regular phone sex with him. He admitted that he's in a committed relationship but, unlike me, she's unwilling to talk about sex freely. "Will you tell her about what you're doing?" I asked. "No," he stammered. "Then you'll be betraying her," I replied. "I could never agree to that." But this is by no means the end of the story. I imagine that this man will continue to approach women until he finds a cooperative one.[3] Frustrated desire doesn't disappear; it intensifies. Eventually he will betray his "significant other."

A betrayer may feel so strangled in a relationship that he honestly believes he must go outside it for the sake of his health. Daniel, a computer software specialist, has an extremely dominating and talkative wife. Whenever he speaks, she interrupts him. All of the details of their daily routine are decided by her; she takes great pride in telling everyone around her, including Daniel, "Make no mistake, I'm the captain of this ship." Daniel doesn't betray his wife. Instead, he puts up with her controlling behavior and stays in the marriage because of his strong religious beliefs and his low self-esteem. Now Daniel has a terminal illness. Literally he's dying inside. Could his relationship be making him sick and extinguishing his will to live? Possibly. Another person might have betrayed to save his own life.

Might your betrayer be feeling an urgent need to escape from what he perceives as oppression?

[3.] In *The Erotic Mind* (New York, HarperPerennial, 1996), Jack Morin, Ph.D., argues that erotic desire actually flourishes in the presence of obstacles to its fulfillment.

BETRAYAL IS ABOUT SEEKING LOVE

It's what the world needs most and what everybody wants: L-O-V-E. If you feel cherished and special, it's unlikely you'll betray your partner; if you don't, you very well may. A loveless relationship is fertile soil for a secret, outside relationship, no matter how strict the couple's moral standards are. Emily has been in a physically abusive marriage for ten years. Her father used to beat her as well. One Sunday afternoon she met Frederick, a chiropractor, at a friend's wedding. He called her up, and he started visiting her. Frederick treated her with caring and respect, things she'd never experienced before. Emily could hardly believe what is happening to her. All of a sudden her religious convictions, her marriage vows, and her responsibilities as a mother of two children took second place. She had to keep her relationship with Frederick (who himself is married and the father of a one-year-old son), even if it meant betraying her husband.

Is it possible that your betrayer is desperately seeking love that he feels he is not getting from you?

BETRAYAL IS ABOUT A HURT EGO

The reason for your betrayal may be very simple: Your partner may be feeling slighted. All of us need regular praise so that we feel valued and important. A little appreciation goes a long way. But once we get married, we tend to take each other for granted; instead of expressing gratitude to our partner, we expect him to fulfill our needs.

When I ask betrayers, "Why did you do it?" at least half tell me they feel that their partner has betrayed them first. In their view they are retaliating for their own heartbreak. Glenn, a professional athlete, insists, "My wife kicked me out of bed the year before I betrayed her."

I learned later that Charles had left me and our three babies because he felt I had betrayed him. When we got married, he believed that he would always be the center of my attention and receive my undivided love. After the children were born, I became ill and so was unable to fuss over him the way I used to. Our time together became less romantic, our sex life became hurried, and our evenings out became less frequent. It was even difficult for me to make him his usual sandwiches to take to work when three little mouths were screaming for oatmeal. Where was the sex kitten, the charming date, and the loving caretaker he married? She had become a "mom," preoccupied with nursing her babies instead of pleasing him. To Charles, this was an enormous disappointment. He hurt so much that he couldn't even talk about it. Besides, what good would a discussion do? As he saw it, nothing was going to change. Because he felt betrayed, he betrayed me. A person with a starving ego is ready to give away his heart to anyone who feeds it.

Ask yourself, "Have I neglected to give my betrayer the day-to-day ego support he needs?"

BETRAYAL IS ABOUT UNFULFILLED FANTASIES

Each of us has a perfect partner whom we dream of. Of course, no one person can fulfill all our fantasies: a sexual god, substitute therapist, spiritual guide, soothing parent, adorable playmate, and stable homebody. These roles can be contradictory, and we may be comfortable playing one more than another.

You fulfill some of your partner's ideals but not all of them. Your partner knows your faults, flaws, and foibles and has no illusions that you're perfect. So it's difficult for him to fantasize about you—and easier for him to fantasize about someone he hardly knows.

Now that women work outside the home, the opportunities for meeting other potential partners are virtually unlimited. The two sexes mingle freely with each other: We have business lunches, attend meetings, and work together late at the office. We get to know an array of people—including some who are sexually attractive. One day we may encounter one who appears to match our fantasy. His looks, personality, and sexual persona are exactly what we've been dreaming about.

If our conversation gets personal, we may continue it outside the office, in person, on the phone, or even on the Internet. Sooner or later we start talking about sex. We share sexual fantasies; we may even act them out. A fire is ignited that cannot be quenched. The new person, whom we hardly know, seems to manifest our ideal vision; our partner, with whom we are extremely familiar, does not. The seeds of a betrayal have been sown.

Could your betrayer be fulfilling a lifelong fantasy?

BETRAYAL IS ABOUT UNACKNOWLEDGED CHANGES

In the heat of romantic infatuation we make promises to each other, sometimes explicitly, sometimes implicitly: "I will always love you exactly as you are." "I will always be who [I think] I am right now." "Sex between the two of us will always be as ecstatic as it is tonight." "Never will I want to make love to anyone else but you." While all of these statements ring true at the moment they are made, they are unrealistic in the long run. I will change. You will change. We'll both do things that will turn each other off sexually: wear dirty sweatshirts, forget to shower, or gain twenty pounds. We'll get bored with whatever excites us sexually now if we do it often enough. Each of us will start to fantasize about having sex with other people. And one or both of us actually may do it.

Love, like life, is dynamic. As much as you would like for you and your partner to remain the same, you don't. The man you married when you were twenty-seven isn't the same person fifteen years later. Neither are you. The gap between you is so enormous that neither of you can connect with the other's life experience anymore. The relationship has lost its promise. Love has died.

In a betrayal these changes aren't acknowledged. You don't openly communicate about your disappointments: "We have nothing in common except maybe the kids and the household budget. I want to break out of our routine—vacation in a different place, meet new people, experiment with sexual techniques we haven't yet tried." Neither of you acknowledges what's been going on; you pretend that everything's still the same and go through the motions of daily living.

While betrayals can happen anytime, they typically take place after a major life change. This includes the birth of a baby, the last child leaving home, a midlife crisis, female or male menopause,[4] a serious illness, the loss of a job, and retirement. Many people who turn forty or fifty or even sixty experience a midlife crisis that propels them to pursue their unfulfilled dreams. The result can be a sports car, a drastic career change—or a relationship betrayal.

[4.] For an excellent discussion of male menopause, see Jed Diamond, *Male Menopause*, Naperville, Illinois, Sourcebooks, 1997.

No matter what the life change, the dynamic is the same. The person experiencing an inner shift doesn't feel connected to—or supported by—his partner. Driven to get his needs met, the betrayer seeks satisfaction elsewhere.

Could there have been a major, unacknowledged change that led your partner to betray you?

BETRAYAL IS ABOUT HIDDEN TRUTHS

Which of us can say we fully know ourselves? Our search for who we really are is lifelong. It slows down when we are preoccupied with family and work responsibilities, and it intensifies when we have the leisure to pursue it. It is accelerated when we attend a personal growth seminar, listen to tapes, or read books that enable our inner voice to speak to us.

What do we find out as we explore our inner depths? Lots of surprises. About work: "I hold an office job but I'd rather be a poet." Or "I'm tired of being a homemaker; I want to brush up on my massage skills and start my own business." About sex: "I'd like to experience sex in new positions, on the phone, in a public place, etc." About money and lifestyle: "I don't need the big house, the two cars, the television sets, the computer—all the expensive 'stuff' I have. I'd like to sell it and buy a mobile home." Or "I want to live all by myself." About emotions: "I'd like a relationship in which my partner and I could be totally honest and up-front with each other, even when we're attracted to other people." Or "I'd love to go somewhere secluded, take off all my clothes, and whoop, holler, and scream for a couple of hours. Would you like to come along?"

Your partner can't be faulted for not being honest with you if he hasn't known his real self up to now. It takes a long time to connect with the unique and special person who you are. Once your partner begins his inner journey, he confronts a dilemma: "Shall I reveal what I am learning about myself? Will you be supportive or critical?" If your response is "How dare you think of leaving your job, adopting a child, or even sharing your deep feelings?" he'll be deeply hurt. By revealing what he's hidden from himself, he may lose the relationship he cherishes the most.

Unacknowledged sexual changes often lead to a betrayal. Your partner desires a sexual experience the two of you have never had before: "I'd like to make love next to our hot tub, on the beach, or in your office." "I think I'd enjoy receiving oral sex for a change, not just giving it." "What about our having an open marriage?"

Talking about sex is difficult for many people. At first your partner's message may sound shocking and awkward as he struggles to express himself. It may seem like criticism, but it's actually a cry for help. What your partner is really saying is this: "I've never admitted this to myself before (let alone to you), but I've finally realized that I want to have a different kind of sex (oral sex, anal sex, phone sex, cybersex)." Or "I feel frustrated with our sex life. The reason we don't have sex as often as you'd like is that I'm bored with the same old routine." Or "What used to satisfy me sexually doesn't anymore. How about exploring some new techniques?"

Your partner may decide to disclose bit by bit. Perhaps he mentions that he's unhappy at work, that he just read an article about how sharing intimate feelings improves your marriage, or that a friend told him about sex on the Internet. Or he may not share his self-discovery at all. Maybe it's not even that he's terrified; he simply doesn't know how. But here's the catch: If your partner conceals what's going on within, he's a walking time bomb. His hidden feelings and needs will intensify. If someone else comes along with whom he can comfortably communicate this information, there is an instant bond of understanding. The relationship can move from a casual conversation to an intimate friendship to a love affair to a sexual liaison. Inadvertently your partner has betrayed you.

Could your partner have recently discovered a deep inner need that he now yearns to fulfill?

BETRAYAL IS ABOUT SUBSTANCE ADDICTION

Someone who is addicted to alcohol or drugs is more likely to betray than someone who is not. An addict has a one-track mind. If he does not feel that you support his habit, he will go outside the relationship to find someone else who does. Gene tells me, "My spouse used to smoke marijuana with me when we first met but eventually she stopped. When I met someone else who enjoyed sitting down with me, watching David Letterman, and smoking a joint, I finally felt comfortable again. Hillary accepted my habit. I didn't have to smoke in the bathroom or hide my supply. It didn't take long before we were sneaking around together."

Other people find solace in a drinking buddy, especially if their partner is judgmental about their addiction. Yes, you're right to request that your partner join a twelve-step program such as Alcoholics Anonymous or go to a detox center, but you may alienate him at the same time. An unsympathetic partner and an eager new addict-friend is a recipe for betrayal.

Is your partner an addict? Could this be why he betrayed you?

BETRAYAL IS ABOUT BECOMING (OR NOT BECOMING) A PARENT

When it comes to children, most of us have an agenda. Some people don't want children at all. Perhaps they had an unhappy childhood they don't want to repeat, prefer to avoid eighteen years of personal and financial responsibility, or choose not to add to the overpopulation of the world. To other people, having offspring is the *raison d'être* of their lives. Many men still yearn for a child to carry on the family name; many women crave the experience of pregnancy and childbirth. To some betrayers, the gender of the child is critically important; they seek someone who already has a boy or a girl—or who is willing to try for one.

When parenting preferences are not agreed upon initially, or when one person changes his mind about parenting, betrayal is likely. The dissatisfied person is powerfully motivated to go outside the relationship for biological satisfaction.

Is it possible that your betrayer may have wanted a baby (when you didn't) or preferred to avoid parenthood (when you didn't)?

Prescription for Betrayal Prevention

If you're thinking that I've been giving you a formula for recognizing—and preventing—betrayals, you're right. While not infallible, here is betrayal insurance worth far more to you than the cost of this book.

At least twice a year, ask yourself these important questions:

1. *Who is my partner really? Why was I attracted to him? What makes him unique and special, different from everyone else I've ever met? How can I use this information to strengthen our bond?*
2. *Is my partner harboring resentment? If so, how can we get it out in the open?*

3. *Is power equally shared in our relationship? Could my partner be feeling powerless? If so, what can I do to rebalance our power?*
4. *What are my partner's deepest emotional needs? Am I fulfilling them? If not, how can we become more intimate?*
5. *Do my partner and I share a common spiritual bond? If not, should we create one?*
6. *Is my partner trying to tell me about how he's changed? Am I really listening?*
7. *Does my partner feel trapped in our relationship? If so, what can I do to ease the pressure?*
8. *Have the two of us honestly discussed and reached agreement about our current parenting needs? If not, when can we begin?*
9. *Have I recently asked my partner whether or not he is satisfied with our sex life? If not, when can I initiate a dialogue?*
10. *If my partner is abusing drugs or alcohol, how am I dealing with it? Am I maximizing or minimizing the chances of a betrayal?*

If you have not been betrayed, knowing the most common causes may enable you to avoid a devastating experience. While I cannot guarantee that a betrayal will never happen to you, chances diminish as your awareness of your partner's unique needs and feelings increases.

Portrait of a Typical Betrayal

Dr. Norman Goldner and Dr. Carol Rhodes, marriage counselors and authors of *Why Women and Men Don't Get Along*, paint a vivid picture of how and why a betrayal usually happens.[5] Does any of it sound familiar to you now?

- Your betrayer is dissatisfied with certain aspects of your relationship.
- He calls them to your attention a few times; you seem not to respond.

[5.] *Why Women and Men Don't Get Along*, Troy, Michigan, Somerset Publishing, 1992. This vignette is based on a "Relationship Corner" column of theirs in the *Troy-Somerset Gazette*, August 7, 1996.

- Your betrayer's frustration builds because he feels ignored.
- Eventually he gives up. He becomes sullen, even depressed.
- You don't notice how upset your betrayer really is.
- He shifts his energy and emotions away from you.

At this point the betrayal is an accident waiting to happen. Your partner is open to connecting with any attractive person who offers attention, understanding, and responsiveness. His new friend appears caring, empathetic, and exciting—very different from you.

The scenario continues:

- Your betrayer makes a deliberate choice to direct his energy and emotions toward his new friend. Their relationship deepens and becomes sexual.
- He makes another deliberate choice not to tell you. He and his new friend start to plan their future together.
- You are unaware of what is going on. He has formed another relationship right under your nose.

At some point you find out what's going on. You urge your betrayer to go for counseling but he refuses. After all he's been distancing himself from you emotionally and sexually for months or even years. There's no way he's going to go backward. He's found what he's looking for and is not about to give it up.

The betrayal is now a *fait accompli*. Your relationship is unofficially over.

What can you do? Ask your betrayer why he pulled away. He may not tell you what you want to hear, but it's useful information. You can learn something from your betrayal and avoid another similar experience in your next relationship. Even more important, turn your attention to yourself. What are your own hopes, dreams, and fantasies? Aren't you free to realize them? *Now is the time to move forward in your own life.*

Remember, Act III of the drama is "Betrayal Is a Wake-Up Call." The first scene is about dealing with the immediate fallout, and the second scene is about rebuilding your life. Remember, you are the star of your own show. *You have the power to create yourself exactly how you want to be.*

Chapter 6

Rebuild Your Life

etrayal is a fact of life. Yet afterward you don't know what to do. You don't have the information and the skills you need to cope with it. Besides, you don't want just to tread water; you want to swim. Your challenge is, "How can I emerge a stronger person than I was before?" Your betrayal doesn't have to be a disaster; it can be a gateway to personal growth and new opportunities.

Betrayal Is a Wake-Up Call

When you are betrayed you receive a special kind of message. The more shocking, disillusioning, and painful the betrayal, the more important the message. It's about you, not about the betrayer or the accomplice. Life is hitting you over the head with a thunderbolt to tell you something: Your present situation isn't working. It needs an overhaul. Now is the time to take a good, hard look at yourself. What can you learn from this experience? Betrayal is an opportunity not only for self-examination but also to look at your relationships with others.

FROM VICTIM TO VICTORY

Staying a victim is tempting, but it is self-defeating in the long run. At first you feel pathetic, bitter, and afraid. One minute you blame your betrayer, the next minute you hate his accomplice. Yet you don't want these emotions to consume you. To survive, you must move forward. The child within you wants to wallow in self-pity, and the parent within you wants to care for you and help you heal. Who will win the struggle, your child or your parent?

The best revenge is living your life well: experiencing joy and fulfilling your potential. To do this, you must master your fears; take risks;

and above all, continue to love. The surest sign of rebuilding is that you start asking yourself, "How can I let love back into my life?"

FALL IN LOVE WITH YOURSELF

All your life you've been falling in love with other people; now is the time to fall in love with yourself. You're a diamond. Don't put yourself into a setting of scrap metal. How about platinum or gold scattered with precious stones? Every moment is a chance to lavish caring and appreciation on yourself. You may have invested so much of yourself into the relationship with your betrayer that you don't even know who you are.

After a betrayal, you have time alone. This is a precious gift. You reclaim your room; you sleep by yourself. No other adult regularly demands sex, food, or attention. You tune into your own voice, not someone else's. You ask yourself, "What am I feeling now? What do I want? What's right for me?" As you learn to meet your own needs, your freedom is born. You masturbate when you wake up, eat cherries for lunch, and write in your journal late into the night. After hours you can wear what you like, bask in your own energy, and please yourself. You aren't stuck in the old patterns of relating: wearing a mask, pretending to be someone you're not, pleasing someone else. Your direction comes from within, not from without. Slowly you re-create you.

Affirmations like these can speed you on your path:

- *Self-love, self-respect, and self-confidence are my birthright.*
- *I embrace my own power now.*
- *The light in me is setting me free.*
- *I am creating happiness, harmony, and joy in my life.*

Strategies for Survival

Once you have embraced your "self," your relationships with others become different. If you can meet your own emotional, sexual, and financial needs, you have commitments to other people but not attachments. You enjoy being with others but you don't depend on them for your survival.

Affirmations like these can help you define your new way of connecting:

- *I take care of myself now.*
- *I handle my own emotions.*
- *I meet my own sexual needs.*
- *I earn enough money to support myself.*
- *I have the right to an honest relationship.*
- *I am entitled to be treated with love and respect.*

Victory Comes by Agonizing Inches

A long time ago, I read an article about a mother who taught her paralyzed child to walk. It took time, patience, and persistence. I kept repeating one sentence of hers to myself during each of my betrayals: "Victory comes by agonizing inches."[1] Rebuilding your life is a series of small victories, too. Altogether, there are ten. They don't necessarily happen in the sequence I describe here, but they very well may.

THE FIRST VICTORY: ACCEPT WHAT HAPPENED

On the wall of a good friend of mine is a framed picture that contains this paragraph: "Acceptance is the answer to all my problems today. When I am disturbed it is because I find some person, place, thing, or situation—some fact of my life—unacceptable to me, and I can find no serenity until I accept that person, place, thing or situation as being exactly the way it is supposed to be at this moment. Nothing, absolutely nothing happens in God's world by mistake."[2]

Once you accept your betrayal you can hear its message: God (or fate) has rerouted you to a new path. No matter how bleak everything looks right now it's part of God's (or fate's) plan for you and there's nothing you can do to erase it from your life. You're upset, you're frightened, but you're standing in the doorway to a bright future. Accept it; eventually you will welcome it.

---

[1] Mrs. William Rotter, "A Young Mother's Story: I Left My Newborn Son to Die," *Redbook*, October, 1972, p. 50.
[2] *Big Book*, Alcoholics Anonymous, p. 402.

Never mind what will become of your betrayer and his accomplice. Don't waste your time thinking about the two of them being happy together. It may or may not happen—and if it does it may not last for long. Three years from now you may be the most joyous one of all. Impossible as it may seem right now you may actually want to send flowers to the accomplice with a note, "Thanks for taking my betrayer off my hands." But right now this is not your concern. What you need to be focusing on is, "What's going to become of me?"

THE SECOND VICTORY: DEAL WITH THE EMOTIONAL TRAUMA

A mega-betrayal is a trauma—a shocking, surprising, and frightening experience. After the moment of the initial shock you feel stuck, frozen, and unable to access your inner resources. You feel angry, sad, hurt, and guilty. Because you have suddenly lost something precious you fear it may happen again. You waste a lot of energy suppressing your negative emotions and limiting beliefs. In all likelihood you will remain in this weakened state until the imprint of the trauma is released.

Dr. Judith Swack, a research biochemist and neurolinguistic programmer, has developed a successful method for dealing with traumas. You can learn it easily and do it alone in the privacy of your own home. It consists of using the Callahan Technique™ for phobias and simple muscle tests derived from the principles of applied kinesiology.

I used Dr. Swack's method to clear not only my mega-betrayal with Buddy but also other traumas that had happened earlier in my life. It really works. If you want to use it, too, send for a copy of her article "The Basic Structure of Loss and Violence Trauma Imprints."[3] For her procedure to work effectively, you must follow her exact instructions.

Journal writing is another helpful way to deal with the trauma of betrayal. Every day as soon as you wake up, write down your feelings about what's happening: what is upsetting to you, what you need that

---

[3.] "The Basic Structure of Loss and Violence Trauma Imprints," *Anchor Point*, March, 1994, p. 1. For a copy of this article and information about her workshops, write to Judith Swack & Associates at 400 Hillside Avenue, Needham, Massachusetts 02194. Dr. Swack and her associates are also available for in-person and telephone consultations.

you aren't getting, and what you need that you are going to ask for. Your journal doesn't have to be a literary masterpiece; just allow whatever comes up to flow through your pen onto your paper. If you prefer, talk into a tape recorder.

THE THIRD VICTORY: REALIZE YOUR INNER STRENGTH

During one of my darkest moments a cherished friend left a message on my answering machine that I played again and again: "You've got the strength to get through this. You're a tough person. Remember, life is in session now. We're here to learn and to grow. We amaze ourselves at how strong we are and how we can stay intact through the worst of times."

My friend is right. You have within you enormous inner strength, which you can tap into at any time. It's like an emergency savings account; you don't need it when your life is sailing along, but when a crisis hits it's available for you to use.

The problem is that in the aftermath of a betrayal your self-confidence is in the ego shredder. Your partner has been making powerful negative statements: "You're no longer number one in my world. You're not sexually desirable anymore. You don't deserve my honesty." *But you don't have to believe these messages.* When they're beamed at you, you can say aloud to your betrayer or whisper to yourself, "Who cares. So what if I'm number two with you?" Or "That's not true. Maybe I'm not attractive to you anymore but I am still sexy." Or "Nonsense. I am worthy of being told the truth." Your healthy inner voice can drown out the static outside.

In all likelihood you have already survived other crises besides this betrayal. Take an inventory of your personal strengths. List the situations in which you have been down and out: illness, financial reversals, and the loss of loved ones. Did you overcome each one? How? Most likely you have shown resilience. What can you learn from these experiences that you can apply to your situation now?

After my second betrayal, I continued to reach for my healthy voice every day. I repeated these affirmations from *A Course in Miracles®* at least once a day:

- *I am entitled to miracles.*
- *God is the strength in which I trust.*

- *I am the light of the world.*
- *Only God's plan for salvation will work.*
- *To give and to receive are one in truth.*[4]

I also created ten other affirmations myself. Upon awakening every day, I said each one three times:

- *I awaken in gratitude and appreciation.*
- *I am a healthy person.*
- *I am entitled to joy.*
- *I have the right to sexual pleasure.*
- *I am entitled to do work that I love.*
- *I have the right to get paid what I'm worth.*
- *I am entitled to prosperity and abundance.*
- *I am entitled to a lasting, loving relationship.*
- *I have confidence in myself.*
- *I have faith in God.*

As I said each sentence to myself I felt courage seep through my veins. It took no more than ten minutes each day—and it enabled me to get through the other twenty-three hours and fifty minutes.

Besides mental, emotional, and spiritual strength you have physical stamina. Never mind your structure—deep within is the endurance you need to get through this crisis.

It is critical that you take extra-good care of your body after a betrayal. It is tempting to eat junk food, skip meals, postpone exercise, or go without sleep. These habits will deplete your energy. I recommend instead that you deliberately take extra time and spend a bit more money to make your body stronger.

Increasing your physical strength can be described in simple arithmetic:

- Subtract red meat and chicken from your diet.
- Add one or two extra salads a day.

---

4. Helen Schucman and William Thetford, *A Course in Miracles*®, Mill Valley, CA, Foundation for Inner Peace, Inc., 1975, Lesson 77 (p. 127), Lesson 47 (p. 75), Lesson 61 (p. 102), Lesson 71 (p. 121), and Lesson 108 (p. 195).

- Subtract potato chips, cookies, and cake from your diet.
- Add several pieces of fresh fruit.
- Subtract soft drinks and coffee from your diet.
- Add "the drink."

What is "the drink?" In a blender combine:

- Three types of fresh fruit (for example, a banana, a peeled grapefruit, and six strawberries)
- A dozen nuts (raw almonds are best)
- Six pieces of dried fruit (pitted dates are sensational)
- One teaspoon of bee pollen (if you're not allergic)
- One teaspoon of powdered brewer's yeast (available at most health food stores)
- Two teaspoons of wheat germ
- Three teaspoons of oat bran
- Any other nutrients you desire

Blend on high speed for two minutes. Half a pitcher of "the drink" in the morning will give you enough energy to last until mid-afternoon.

You also need to find at least fifteen minutes a day to exercise. Ride a bike, walk your dog, use exercise equipment, do aerobics—whatever you enjoy. Movement doesn't make you tired; it invigorates you. This vital information will help you to stay physically strong and to avoid constant exhaustion and irritability during the aftermath of your betrayal.

THE FOURTH VICTORY: ASSESS YOUR RESOURCES

Immediately after a betrayal you feel devastated. You've lost trust; you've been abandoned; you feel like there's nothing left. But a month or two later you start asking, "What can I salvage from this betrayal?" You open your eyes and realize, "I may have lost my lover but I still have me."

The secret of rebuilding your life is to focus on what you have, not on what you don't. Believe it or not you have a wide range of resources to call upon as you begin to create your new life. Make an inventory of them now. Which of the following resources do you have in abundance?

- *Emotional: self-esteem, self-respect, self-confidence*
- *Physical: strength, flexibility, endurance*
- *Mental: intelligence, intuition, creativity*

- *Spiritual: forgiveness, faith, feeling connected to a power greater than yourself*
- *Financial: income from a career or a job, real estate, savings and investments, personal property*
- *Temporal: youth, lots of spare time*
- *Social: friends, relatives, connections with interesting or influential people*

You may have more of one resource than another. For example, I had powerful social resources but limited financial ones. Assessing your resources is a necessary preliminary step in making your plan to rebuild your life.

THE FIFTH VICTORY: MAKE A PLAN

Your plan doesn't necessarily appear quickly, neatly, and completely. You decide to make it and then wait for bits and pieces to arrive. Remember, you're not thinking clearly yet. After the betrayal you feel afraid and uncertain. That's normal. Stay in your confusion. It's okay not to understand where you are supposed to be going. You don't need to know how everything is going to turn out in the end. Saying, "I don't know," is part of the process of self-discovery. At least you're in dialogue with yourself. You will know what you need to know when you need to know it.

My plan has two parts: a daily routine and a long-term vision. My days are building blocks of the vision but they have a direction of their own.

I saw the aftermath of my second betrayal as an opportunity to reorder my priorities and reapportion my time. I stopped doing activities I didn't enjoy, such as cooking elaborate vegetarian meals and walking my dogs the same route every day. I started eating fresh fruits and vegetables, taking the dogs to new neighborhoods for walks, and spending the extra time on my grooming and mental conditioning.

Although your daily routine is uniquely yours, there are common guidelines:

- *Care for your health.* You've heard it before: Diet and exercise *are* the keys. What you eat determines what you weigh. I've always exercised, but my body shape remained the same: chubby thighs, round backside, oversized waist. The week after

Buddy left I threw out all the fattening cooked food in the refrigerator that we used to eat when we were together. I started eating salads and drinking fresh-squeezed juice instead. In less than three months I lost thirty pounds. Yes, it cost money to buy new clothes, but it was worth it. How I enjoyed my thin, healthy body!

- *Take the time to look your best.* The most valuable advice I ever received during my betrayal was from a beautiful travel agent in her sixties: "When you wake up in the morning put on your nicest clothes, fix your hair, and put on makeup. When you look in the mirror you'll like what you see. It doesn't matter if no one else sees you; you're looking good for yourself. When other people do look at you they'll respond to your attractiveness and reflect it back."

- *Do at least one service for others every day.* When you do something for others you feel good about yourself. As an added bonus, you inspire them to do the same. It's not a "tit for tat" proposition; I do this and then you do that. Your positive energy is contagious. When you assist other people, they are moved to support you. For example, while I was struggling financially after my betrayal, I learned about a computer dating service that needed relationship coaches. After I signed on I recommended three of my colleagues for the same position. Perhaps it was no coincidence that later on two of them took an active interest in helping *me* make money.

- *Read at least one inspiring passage from a book or listen to a motivational tape at least once a day.* Twice a day is best— immediately upon arising and right before you go to bed—but if you're pressed for time, mornings are best. If you're not sure what book to read, see the list at the back of this book for suggestions and pick whatever suits your taste.

- *Talk to at least one upbeat person every day.* Catch their energy. There's nothing that can pull you out of the doldrums better than someone else's enthusiasm. It can be someone you know or a complete stranger with whom you make a positive connection. After my betrayal I learned how to establish rapport with telemarketers, secretaries, and airline ticket agents. Often I'd end a conversation thinking I'd made a new friend, even if just for a few moments. Of course, I relied on people I knew well to be consistently upbeat.

- *Take a trip.* Getting away from your daily stress and responsibilities can work wonders. Take a weekend or a week. Your trip is not a drain on your time; it's an investment in using your time more efficiently. The better you feel, the more you can do. If you can't afford to leave town, then vacation in your neighborhood. Go to a park, a beach, a museum, a shopping mall, or some other place you've never been. Another option is to take your phone off the hook, leave your mail in the mailbox, and take a "home vacation." Whatever your preference, you'll break away from the daily grind.

- *Do at least three nice things for yourself every day.* A woman named Alice taught me a lesson I will always remember. Alice was a powerful, self-confident person with an inner beauty that shined through to everyone she met. When I asked her, "What is your secret?" she replied, "I make it a habit to do at least three nice things for myself every day." I take a bubble bath, I get a massage, I eat a piece of delicious fruit, I call a good friend on the phone—whatever makes me happy at the time. Before I take care of anyone else, I care for myself." Put yourself first. Self-care is the pathway to mental and physical health.

- *Streamline your days so you spend less time on unnecessary tasks and more time nurturing yourself and other people.* While I was healing, I was privileged to attend a seminar at the Esalen Institute conducted by renowned group leader David Schiffman. It was called "The Simple Life."[5] What magic it was! Clearing items out of my home was the first task. I threw away useless papers, gave away old clothes, and donated furniture and household items to charity. If I hadn't

---

[5.] "The Simple Life" is a weekend seminar regularly given at the Esalen Institute, Big Sur, California 93920. Write to Esalen for a complete catalog of their weekend and five-day classes.

used something during the past year, out it went. It was a chance for me to define exactly what was valuable to me. My outer cleaning was a catalyst for my inner, mental cleaning. As I took an inventory of the things that remained, I asked myself, "What thoughts, feelings, and ideas of mine do I cherish as well? Which irrelevant ones do I want to discard?"

Your long-term vision will soon appear. It usually involves making big changes in your life. And it may require taking risks. And risk taking—whether financial or romantic—can be frightening. It is natural to be afraid of doing something you've never done before, but you can't let your concerns hold you back. As long as you are not attached to one particular result, you will benefit from your risk. Asking, "What will happen if . . ." helps you prepare yourself for a possible negative outcome. Saying, "I don't know what will happen so I'd better not try" keeps you from a positive one. If you get stuck in F-E-A-R (False Events Appearing Real),[6] you will never get to the L-O-V-E (Lots Of Vital Energy) that's waiting for you.

Ask yourself, "What opportunities does this betrayal open up for me? What new directions can I take that I've always wanted to take? How can I achieve true success—doing what I love?" Your long-term vision is not about what you should do, how you should look, or how you should behave. It's about what you've always wanted to do and how you yearn to look, feel, and relate to others. Now is the time to discover how you visualize your ideal:

- *Career.* Do you want to remain in the same job? If not, what kind of new employment are you looking for? Do you want to work longer hours or ease off? Do you want to go work at the same time or change your schedule? Do you want to make substantially more money or are you content to stay at the same salary level?
- *Outside interests.* What have you always wanted to do in your spare time? Read, write, listen to music, learn to play a musical instrument, start skydiving lessons, study flower arranging, take a class in auto mechanics, or sit on the beach?

[6.] My cherished literary agent and friend, Susan Crawford, taught me this one.

- *Vacations.* Where have you always wanted to go? How can you get there (by car, by bus, or with accumulated miles on an airline)? How much will it cost? How long will it take you to save the money for your trip? One woman I know couldn't wait long; she took a chunk of the money she already had, bought airline tickets, and traveled around the world. A lifetime dream of hers was fulfilled.

- *Friends.* With whom do you enjoy spending time? Remember, friendship is about pleasure, not about obligation. Make a list with two columns, one headed "friends I want to keep" and the other headed "people who don't belong in my life." Then with compassion and politeness begin to distance yourself from the latter. I do this once a year. It enables me to recognize uncomfortable relationships. I regularly exit from them just as I weed my garden and clean out my closet.

- *Romantic partner.* With whom are you emotionally and sexually intimate? It doesn't have to be someone other than yourself. Whether or not you have a partner, you are a complete person. If you're unattached, spend some time deciding who you're looking for. Write down the ideal characteristics of your ideal partner. (Someone who doesn't betray you might be a good start.) My list was short: "great sex, good fun, and someone who can support himself."

- *Sexual style.* After a betrayal is a good time to do a sexual inventory. What sexual experiences have you been longing to have? What sexual fantasies do you dream of fulfilling? What romantic turn-ons do you yearn for? If you could not express your authentic sexual style in your previous relationship, you are free to do so now. Between two consenting adults, anything goes.

- *Place to live.* One of the best ways I know to liberate yourself from the painful memories of a betrayal is to "leave the scene of the crime." It liberates you from old habits—and painful memories. If you can possibly manage it, move to a new home or even a new city. If you can't leave, consider redecorating, or at the very least rearranging some furniture and buying wall hangings (you can find excellent second-hand ones at garage sales) to give your residence a new look.

My long-term plan involved a complete change in lifestyle; yours may not. After my betrayal I experienced a total transformation. I became Riki Robbins (my maiden name), moved to Northern California, became single, started dating, trained as a sex therapist, watched my two sons become financially independent, distanced myself from old friends, and made brand-new ones. In one year I changed my name, my address, my phone number, my marital status, my sexual style, my career direction, and my relationships with people I loved. My plan was a series of guideposts that allowed room for deviations (and surprises!) every step of the way.

THE SIXTH VICTORY: ASK YOURSELF FOUR TOUGH QUESTIONS

None of us like to have a confrontation, especially with ourselves. But it's necessary in the aftermath of a betrayal. When it comes to rebuilding your life, denial can be deadly. Your challenge is not only to ask yourself these four questions but also to come up with answers that work for you:

1. *With whom will I spend weekends and holidays?* Possible answers include: my kids, when they're available; members of my extended family; my pets; old friends; new friends; God; myself.
2. *Who will help me with the housework? With yard work? With child care?* Possible answers include: my children; my family members; an old friend; a new friend; someone I pay.
3. *How will I support myself financially?* Possible answers include: get an extra job; find a different job; change careers; start a home-based business.
4. *How will I handle my sex drive?* Possible answers include: abstain from sex; masturbate; use a vibrator; enjoy sex differently than I have in the past, such as sex without intercourse; be sexual with a different kind of partner, such as trying casual sex or having sex with a friend.

Answer these questions in succession so you don't feel over-whelmed. One a week is more than enough. It takes time to figure out the answers that are right for you. Keep a pencil and paper handy to write down ideas whenever they pop into your mind.

THE SEVENTH VICTORY: CREATE A SUPPORT SYSTEM

You recover from a betrayal quickly when other people help. You may already have a support system of relatives and friends in place. If not, begin to create one. Make a list of:

- People who will talk to you about their betrayal experiences
- People who will listen to yours with empathy
- People who will advise you on practical details
- People who will make you feel loved and special
- People who will cheer you on when you start a new venture

You're used to defending your children, your friends, and causes you believe in. Now is the time to become your own advocate. Ask yourself, "Why am I feeling bad? What do I need to feel better?" Then share your feelings and needs with others. If you don't stand up for yourself, no one else will.

My good friends and colleagues Dr. Judith Sherven and Dr. James Sniechowski gave me a precious gift one afternoon. I had called to tell them I was having financial difficulties and no one seemed to be responding to my calls for help. "What you say determines the response you get," Judith declared. "This is what you must do," James continued. "Ask for exactly what you need. Make a specific request. Not, 'I want you to be there for me,' but 'I need you to come over and watch the kids from 7:00 to 10:00 on Friday evenings so I can take a computer class.'" I started following their suggestions and got all kinds of valuable sup-port. A few precious friends and relatives sent me money; some told me about additional writing opportunities; others gave me advice on how to find other kinds of temporary employment. By tailoring my specific request to what the person might have to offer I allowed each person to "be there" for me in his or her own unique way. Sharing your experi-ence with others who have been betrayed is particularly valuable. While I had no opportunity to exchange information after Charles left, I start-ed listening to other people talk about their betrayals six months before

Buddy confronted me. Then it was their turn to hear my story. If you're not yet connected with others in the same plight, join a betrayal support group or start one of your own. Don't hide behind a smokescreen of embarrassment. We're in this together. Keep on putting it out there! In the next chapter, I will discuss how to give support to someone who has been betrayed.

THE EIGHTH VICTORY: PAY ATTENTION TO YOUR BODY'S MESSAGES

After a betrayal your body usually hurts—someplace. Where is your pain? In *Heal Your Body* Louise Hay presents a complete list of physical discomforts and the mental causes of each one.[7] If you identify your particular illness you can use appropriate affirmations to help heal yourself.

Each part of your body that hurts is sending you a different message. For example, after Charles's betrayal I had severe pain in my lower back. According to Louise Hay, this meant that I had serious financial concerns and was afraid of not having enough money. I needed to affirm that I felt safe that I would be taken care of. Right on! After Buddy betrayed me I developed a knee problem. This meant in Louise's terms that I was experiencing fear and inflexibility because I didn't want to "give in" to him. An affirmation about forgiveness and flowing with ease was in order. Another accurate assessment.

When your body speaks, what is it telling you? Are you listening to it? Can you create an affirmation to address your pain?

THE NINTH VICTORY: BREAK THE INNER BOND WITH YOUR BETRAYER

Betty Ann Thompson, a well-known attorney in Arlington, Virginia shared with me her insight as to why it takes so long for divorcing couples to split up: In spite of the betrayal, the two of you still feel affection toward each other. You and your betrayer continue to hang on to your relationship with the hope that you may reconcile. There is an unspoken inner bond between the two of you that is keeping you together. This is why a couple will continue to fight about small issues: "Who gets Aunt Tilly's teapot?" "You have to send me an extra ten dollars a month!"

[7.] *Heal Your Body*, Carlsbad, California, Hay House, 1988.

"The check was two days late." These are all excuses for keeping communication alive. You can't go your own ways until you're completely separated inside.[8]

To rebuild your life you must cut the cord and move on. Slowly but surely you need to create your own independent life. Do not nourish your emotional and sexual connection to your betrayer. Instead, welcome forces into your life that will diminish it.

Making a transitional connection can be helpful. If the opportunity arises you can become emotionally, and even sexually, involved with someone else temporarily. Even though this person may not be available for a serious relationship, you think about him instead of your betrayer. While I never had sex with my married friend, I directed enormous amounts of emotional energy toward him that otherwise would have been given to Buddy. My transitional connection made it much easier for me to make the final break.

THE TENTH VICTORY: ASK YOURSELF, "WHAT CAN I LEARN FROM THIS?"

Betrayal is a gift. It's not wrapped in elegant paper with a shiny new ribbon; it's packaged in a plain brown paper bag. It's not a glamorous way to learn, but no one ever said life's lessons would be fun.

After a betrayal you have a unique opportunity to examine yourself, your partner, and the relationship the two of you created together. Why were you betrayed? How was your partner unhappy? Were you also uncomfortable? Why? What will you do differently in your next relationship? Will you seek a new partner with other qualities? Which ones?

After Charles left it was easy to figure out the answers: I was betrayed because I had abandoned him emotionally. He was unhappy because I was spending too much time with the children. I was uncomfortable because he didn't share the responsibilities with me. I promised myself I would go out more and get more involved in my next partner's life. I would also seek someone who shared my interest in my kids.

When Buddy betrayed me it was more difficult to figure out what I was supposed to learn. Initially I attributed his betrayal to the appeal

---

[8.] Conversation with the author, March 15, 1996.

of his young accomplice and her son. But after months of soul searching I realized that difficulties in our own relationship had led to the
breakup. Buddy felt that I had been spending more time on my career
than I had with him. I myself had my own discomforts that were never
addressed: our lack of intimacy, our inability to deal with our attractions
to other people, and our over-controlling each other. I promised myself
that the next partner I selected would communicate openly with me
about his feelings and needs and would allow me more freedom. More
important, I committed myself to creating a better balance between
work and personal time and to being more honest about my own feelings and needs. I couldn't undo what I had already done, but I could
learn from my mistakes. So can you. By your example you also become
a teacher to your friends and family.

Family members are deeply affected by a betrayal. For example, my
relationships with my two mother-in-laws were completely different.
Buddy's mother was a constant source of support to me; Charles's
mother sided with him against me. Each of them was agonizing over
what had happened and dealt with her pain in a different way. To
emerge intact from a betrayal, you must rebuild the lives of the other
people involved as well as your own.

Chapter 7

Betrayal Fallout:
Learn to Deal with Relatives and Friends

A mega-betrayal is an event that touches many lives. All of the people around you—your family of origin, your friends, your children, the betrayer's family and friends, and your mutual friends—are affected once they find out what has happened. You, your betrayer, and the accomplice are the main players in the drama of betrayal, but there is also a large supporting cast.

How do family members and friends usually feel after a betrayal? Confused, caught in the middle, hurt, abandoned, indignant, and disappointed. Confused: "I don't understand what's going on." Caught in the middle: "Quincy calls me up and tells me that she's been betrayed, and then Zach comes over and begs me to listen to his story. Whose side do I take?" Hurt and abandoned: "We've just lost two wonderful friends. Now that they're splitting up we'll never see either one of them again." Indignant: "How could this terrible thing have happened? He [the betrayer] is a monster." Disappointed: "They were such a lovely couple. Isn't there anyone left who remains loyal to his wife anymore?"

Relatives and friends feel betrayed just as you do. They trusted both you and your partner. They believed your relationship would last. They had faith that if either of you were unhappy one of you would tell them. In our case, all sixty people who attended our church wedding were asked by our minister to offer their support to me and Buddy in case we ran into relationship difficulties. How could they if they didn't know what was going on? Instead they found out after the betrayal was a *fait accompli*.

There is also a feeling of loss: "Now that they're not a couple anymore we may never see them again. Good-bye to good times. Who are we going to have dinner with on Friday nights? Now we don't have anyone to go on vacation with. I'm really going to miss Irwin's jokes and Patty's bright smile. It's as if we lost our best friends." (And maybe they did.)

How to Communicate with the People You Love

Exactly how do you deal with relatives and friends?

- *Explain clearly exactly what has happened.* You don't have to include every gory detail. Respect their right to know but also be aware of their vulnerability. Parents especially don't appreciate hearing about the errant sexual behavior of their children no matter how old the child may be.
- *Listen to their reactions with empathy.* Now is the time to put your judgmental, analytical tendencies aside and to stay in the realm of feelings. Let them pour out their hearts to you. While you want to protect yourself from being pulled down by their negative energy, you are performing a service when you allow them to vent. Perhaps someday soon they will return the favor.
- *Allow them to be helpful.* Don't slam the door on the people you need the most. If your mom offers to cook for you or your best friend volunteers to babysit, they're doing you a real favor. If you aren't comfortable with what they want to give you, suggest some other appropriate service they can perform.
- *Don't put them in the middle.* Forcing a friend or relative who knows and loves both of you to take your side is tempting but cruel. Let your best bowling buddies or dinner partners make their own decisions about whom they want to stay close with. You may lose some friends, but the ones you'll keep are true.
- *Don't force them to take sides.* They don't understand what happened, and your version may not be 100 percent correct. Your betrayer has his right to share his perspective. To be fair and respectful, allow your friends and relatives to listen to *both* sides and make their own decisions.
- *Reassure them you're okay.* People who care about you *will* worry about you. It's human nature. You don't want cherished friends and relatives losing sleep and fretting unnecessarily. So don't paint a totally bleak picture. If you are upset, be honest but not brutal: "Yes, I'm really hurting about what happened with Oliver, but I'm handling it most of the time. Evenings are the most difficult; perhaps you could call me then." As soon as you're feeling better, let them know.

If You Are a Friend or Relative of a Person Betrayed

WHAT TO DO

If someone you love has been betrayed, what should you do? Here's what helped me the most after my own experiences. I recommend performing one or more of these gestures depending on which are most comfortable for you:

- *Call, send a note, or visit at least once a week.* Don't besiege a betrayed person with hourly or daily phone calls; your hovering will make her think she's worse off than she really is. Your intention is to encourage your friend or relative to feel strong, stand on her own feet, and deal with the situation herself. (If weekly calls or visits are insufficient, the betrayed person is likely in crisis. Make sure that she receives enough support until the crisis is under control. Enlist the help of a psychologist, a psychotherapist, a minister, or a medical doctor if necessary.) Conversely, making a single call or visit and then saying, "That's it—I've done all I need to do," is avoiding the issue. A single Band-Aid is a nice gesture, but it doesn't heal a betrayed person's wound.

- *Share your own betrayal experiences.* Nothing makes a betrayed person feel more soothed than hearing, "I've been through it too, dear." Immediately a common bond is formed between the two of you. Even if the facts of your betrayal are different, your feelings of anger and resentment are the same.

- *Listen sympathetically.* Being a good listener is probably the most welcome gift you can give someone who has been betrayed. But it's not easy to do. Your own feelings of indifference, superiority, fear, despair, blame, and anger may interfere with your ability to really "be there" in spirit.

- *Send a gift: flowers, something nice to eat, bubble bath, a book, or a tape.* Two weeks after I learned that Buddy had betrayed me, the doorbell rang. It was a delivery man with a beautiful pink, red, and white arrangement of carnations and roses. In the middle there was a card that read, "You are loved." Those flowers stayed on my dresser for almost a month and will remain in my heart for a lifetime. The person who had sent them had given me priceless support. A package of fruit, gourmet delectables, or a homemade meal or dessert is another deeply appreciated gesture of support. A soothing gift, such as bubble bath or body lotion, is always welcome. And, of course, a book such as this one (or others listed at the back), or an audio- or videotape can jumpstart the healing of a betrayed friend or relative. Pick a book or a tape you've already benefited from—and one that is appropriate to the particular needs of the person.

- *Offer practical help.* What service can you perform that will make life just a little easier for a betrayed friend or relative in trauma? Perhaps you can offer to help drive the kids to lessons so the person you love can get a little extra rest after a hard day at work. Maybe you can cook dinner one night or else bring over one you're already made. Not nearly so much fun but just as helpful is to come by and help clean the house. Bright and cheery surroundings are a great pick-me-up for anyone who is down.

- *Say, "You can call me anytime, twenty-four hours a day, seven days a week"—and mean it.* At least a dozen people told me this during the aftermath of Buddy's betrayal. I never did phone a single one of them in the middle of the night, but when the panic and loneliness set in at least I knew I *could.* If you honestly can't handle a conversation during the middle of the night, then specify exactly what hours you are available to talk: "I'm in every afternoon between 4:00 and 6:00. Feel free to phone for whatever reason." Let your friend know that whether her need is big or small, you're there to care. "I just needed to hear your voice" is as much a good reason to call as, "I can't stand it one minute longer."

- *Give practical advice.* Your friend or relative may have a variety of brand-new dilemmas, especially if she has been abandoned by her betrayer: "Where can I get my car fixed near home now that I have no one to drive me across town to where I used to go?" "How can I find a good store with attractive second-hand clothes for the kids?" "Do you know how I can use the Internet to find a better job?" Let the betrayed person know your areas of expertise so you can be a resource.

- *Invite the betrayed person out for fun.* "Let's go to the movies"; "Let's have a picnic"; or "Let's spend tomorrow afternoon at the beach" can give your relative or friend a much needed change of pace. Concert tickets, a restaurant discount coupon, or two free passes to an amusement park are all wonderful pick-me-ups. When you're in the midst of disbelief, anger, or grief it's easy to forget the joy in life; shared pleasure and laughter can bring it back.

- *Offer to pray for your betrayed friend or relative.* I always end my conversation with a betrayed person by saying, "I will pray for you." My personal pledge to seek divine support is a reminder that God is with us. If you want to "go the limit," offer to pray for your friend's or relative's betrayer as well. While shocking to some, the truth is that *both* the betrayed person and the betrayer are in need of divine guidance.

WHAT NOT TO DO

Here are some typical dialogues that hurt instead of help.

Dialogue of Indifference
BETRAYED: _____ has been sneaking around. I found out last night.
FRIEND: Yeah? Really?
BETRAYED: Now _____ says _____ wants to leave me for his secretary.
FRIEND: That's life, I guess.
BETRAYED: "It's going to be terrible."
FRIEND: Well, I've got my own problems, too, you know.

Dialogue of Fear
BETRAYED: _____ is leaving me for someone else.
FRIEND: Well, you had better watch out or else you'll lose everything.
BETRAYED: Maybe I can meet someone new, too.
FRIEND: Remember, you're getting old now. You may never find another husband.

Dialogue of Despair
BETRAYED: _____ just told me he's having an affair with a colleague.
FRIEND: You never should have encouraged him to take that job.
BETRAYED: He doesn't want to break it off.
FRIEND: It sounds like your marriage is a mess. I don't envy you. You may never get over it.

Dialogue of Blame
BETRAYED: I just found out that when _____'s been taking all those business trips, _____'s been secretly having sex.
FRIEND: If you hadn't been so busy, always ignoring his needs when he was home, _____ never would have done it. You've taken him for granted, in bed and everywhere else.
BETRAYED: Yeah, our sex life has kind of cooled off, now that I think about it.
FRIEND: If you're good in bed your husband doesn't cheat. You probably didn't please him; I bet that's why it happened.

Dialogue of Anger
BETRAYED: _____ packed his suitcase yesterday. He's going to live with his photography teacher. It seems they've been having sex behind my back for years.
FRIEND: Frankly, you deserve it. You never have time for our friendship and now you ignore your husband. What do you expect?

All of these dialogues add negative energy to the betrayed person's life.

There are five kinds of conversations you should never have:

- *Making light of what happened:* "This too shall pass."
- *Reacting from fear—as if the world has come to an end:* "Oh my God, what are you going to do? This is the worst news I've ever heard."
- *Offering pity:* "Oh, you poor thing."
- *Acting as if you're superior:* "I've never had this problem."
- *Inflicting your own judgments:* "It was all your own fault."

- *Taking sides with the betrayer:* "He had every right to do what he did."

If you're on the receiving end of one of these conversations, you must learn to turn it around to your benefit. You must also teach members of your family of origin and your friends how to talk to you. Here are a few suggestions for responding appropriately:

- "This too shall pass." *"Right now it hurts like heck. I simply can't ignore my pain."*
- "This is the worst news I've ever heard." *"Words of doom and gloom pull me down; they don't lift me up. What I need right now is positive energy."*
- "Oh, you poor thing." *"No one wants to feel pathetic, including me. How about empowering me instead?"*
- "It was all your own fault." *"Of course, it wasn't. I know that."*
- "He had every right to do what he did." *"I really don't feel like getting into an argument. Excuse me, I have to go."*

The most touching expression of caring I received after Buddy left came from a twenty-year-old artist friend of mine. In a calm, reassuring manner he said to me, "Something good will come of this. You are a good and capable person. Things will be okay for you. I know it's tough right now but everything will work out well in the end. Chin up. Call me anytime you need me; I'm here for you."

The five greatest gifts you can offer (and hope to receive) are a matter-of fact, understanding tone of voice; an optimistic, but realistic, attitude; a neutral stance; positive, empowering energy; and sincere and appropriate support.

When Friends and Relatives Betray You

After a betrayal you may assume that certain people will come forth and support you. It is upsetting to find out that they have been secretly loyal to your betrayer and now choose to take sides against you. It is an even greater shock when they are members of your church or synagogue who publicly defend a moral code of fidelity and honesty.

Abraham tells me, "I am an orthodox Jew. When my wife left me for another man, not a single person in our synagogue publicly stood up in my defense. I spoke to several of them privately and they all replied, 'Sorry but I don't want to make waves,' or words to that effect. The truth was they didn't want to antagonize my wife because they wanted to keep her as a synagogue member."

Barbara adds, "My sister-in-law was a Unity minister. She had always acted so lovingly toward me, but when her brother left me for another woman she never said a word. I actually called her and asked her to speak with him on my behalf and she refused. I guess she was more concerned about keeping it quiet and protecting her own reputation than she was about helping me."

The Real Victims: Children of Betrayal

You, your parents, your siblings, and your friends suffer from a betrayal, but your children are hit worst of all. Children of betrayal are caught in the middle. They love both you and your betrayer and want to keep both of you in their lives. Their tragedy is that they're asked to play roles they never wanted:

- *Go-between.* Children of betrayal are caught in the middle. How can they possibly please two people completely at odds with each other? They lie; they pretend; they placate. Often they are forced to take sides. Sometimes they are given messages to convey, and other times they are asked to spy on the betrayer—two roles they should never play.
- *Comforter.* A child of betrayal sees her or his beloved parent hurting. Naturally the child wants to be of comfort. So the child becomes a premature parent. His or her childhood is aborted as the child is unwillingly thrust into adulthood.
- *Surrogate partner.* Single parents particularly encourage this kind of behavior. An other-sex child takes over as head of the family in place of the betrayer. A ten-year-old is asked to give advice, care for siblings, and even be a surrogate romantic partner. What a confusing and difficult role to play!

The salvation of children of betrayal is to spare them your pain and let them live their own lives. This is how you can best support them:

- *Explain what is going on in simple terms.* Children don't need to hear a lot of details about a betrayal; a simple explanation will suffice. "Daddy has found a new friend. They are going to spend a lot of time together and sometimes they will want you to come along. Now you have three people to love you."
- *Protect them from emotional harm.* Don't ask them to take your side against the betrayer, however tempting it is. Don't make them choose between you. Don't say, "Would you rather go to the park with Mom or stay home and play scrabble with Daddy and his new friend?" Instead, say "Today you and I will go to the park; over the weekend you can play with Daddy and his friend." If you openly make choices for them, they won't feel like betrayers.
- *Distance them from the betrayal.* Children of betrayal don't have to witness a confrontation or your betrayer's confession. Find a babysitter, send them to a neighbor's home, or drop them off at a day care center—whatever you need to do to keep them safe. You are protecting them from events they aren't ready to deal with and don't understand.

You need to continue keeping children at a distance from a betrayal long after its initial impact. One child says, "I wish I didn't have to be introduced to every single 'new friend' Daddy has. He changes partners every year. Just when I get attached to her, she and Daddy break up. It hurts."

When you talk to the children of betrayal, do it with love. Understand their fears: that you'll be lonely, broke, or friendless—and that they'll never have a whole family again. A mega-betrayal is disillusioning and painful to a child. One tells me this: "I believed in our family. Who is my family now? I don't know. What's going to happen to me?"

For children of betrayal, your pain is their pain. But you have the power to heal by your example. In your moment of deepest agony, remember that your children, the members of your family of origin, and your friends are all depending on you. As you learn to restore trust, you will show them the way, too.

Chapter 8

Restore Trust:
The Foundation of Love

Trust is the foundation of love. Yet how do you build it? With monotonous regularity you hear your friends and colleagues say, "You can't trust anyone anymore—especially men." Almost every popular magazine you open has an article about how couples cheat on each other. Yes, a majority of married men and women do have sex with someone beside their spouse at least once. And most of them keep it a secret. So what should you conclude? That you're crazy if you trust your partner? Absolutely not.

Ultimately you have to trust someone you love. When you doubt the truth of everything that your partner says, you end up feeling crazy. When you have sex and you have reason to believe your partner's been unfaithful, you feel turned off and upset. Mistrust can make you both physically and mentally sick. To have a healthy approach to life you must believe in someone and something.

Believe in Yourself

Romantic and sexual trust are difficult to establish because they involve both you and another human being. To build a foundation of trust you must lay the bricks at the bottom first. Before you can trust other people, you must choose to believe in yourself. This means knowing yourself, feeling comfortable with yourself, believing you will act in your own best interest, understanding you are capable of protecting yourself from danger, and having confidence in your good judgment. If you already know, love, value, respect, and appreciate who you are, you probably have all five of these crucial attitudes. You can say to yourself, "I know you, I feel safe with you, I can take care of you, I can rely on you, I believe in you"—and mean it. You realize that your primary and fundamental loyalty is always to yourself. You know who you are. You have integrity toward yourself.

Integrity means wholeness. It requires spending time going within to discover and embrace the inner you. Self-knowledge takes courage. Sometimes you may not like what you find. For example, I realize that I have strong masculine traits. Although I am a petite, feminine-looking woman, I am also highly independent, motivated to achieve, and gifted with a strong sex drive. So I don't fit into the traditional stereotype of a woman. Knowing my own strengths and weaknesses enables me to believe in myself. I have confidence that I can establish trusting relationships with people who appreciate my uniqueness.

Trust Your Intuition

To believe in yourself also means to connect with your intuition. Trust is a feeling. You can't describe it exactly, but you know it when you have it. Your inner voice speaks to you and you listen: "This is a good person; trust him" or "Watch out for that person; she's dangerous." Even if other people tell you something opposite, you don't pay attention to anyone else's voice but your own. You have to honor what's inside. "Follow your gut," as a psychiatrist friend once said to me.

Once I answered a personal ad that began, "Lovable Lion. Well-educated, passionate man seeks...." He and I spoke on the phone a couple of times and then met at a restaurant. It turned out that "Lovable Lion" (a Leo by horoscope) was tall, handsome, and charming, and we had a delightful dinner together. Afterward he asked if he could come over to my house for a drink. What should I do? I was extremely attracted to him, but I was also aware that he weighed twice as much as I did and could knock me down with one karate chop. My inner voice said loudly and clearly, "He's safe," so I trusted my instincts and agreed. As we walked up the steps toward my front door I told him about my hesitation. He replied, "Of course you trusted me. You wouldn't have invited me over otherwise." I've experienced this "instant trust" with other lovers as well.

Many couples intuitively trust in each other from the moment they meet. One pair experienced this trust so powerfully that he proposed marriage (and she accepted) on the first date—after they had been together less than six hours. Countless other couples have had sexual relations, confided deeply personal secrets, or been emotionally open right from the start. The seeds of trust germinate and grow when there is powerful initial bonding.

TRUST IS A RISK

You deliberately choose to trust. Just as you can decide to betray someone, you can also decide to give that person your loyalty. Sometimes it's difficult to know what's the right choice. In a world of romantic and sexual chaos, how do you know whom to trust and when? You don't want to follow your impulses blindly. Before you make a decision to trust someone you love, you ask for divine guidance, assess the facts, and—most important—follow your intuition.

Trust is a risk. You feel attracted to someone. What shall you do? Of course, you can always walk away. Or you can let down your guard and say, "I feel comfortable with you. I want to be sexual, to reveal my inner self, to be vulnerable, and to offer my unconditional love." Now you are taking a leap of faith. You don't know the outcome. When you decide to trust someone you open yourself up to joy—and to potential danger.

If you've been betrayed, you can either decide that you can't trust anyone or you can continue to take leaps of faith. If you choose the latter, then be sure to protect yourself. As Ravi Dykema, publisher of *Nexus*, a popular New Age newspaper from Boulder, Colorado puts it, "If you were about to get on a ship and you knew that there was a better than even chance it would sink, wouldn't you interview the captain first? Wouldn't you make sure the life boats were in shape and have a working life preserver with you just in case there was a disaster? The same is true in romantic relationships. If you know that there's a one out of two chance that your marriage will end in divorce, then it makes sense to protect yourself financially, sexually, and emotionally."[1] Always have a fallback position just in case a betrayal happens.

Ultimately, trust requires you to move toward love and away from fear. You choose to stop being afraid of the consequences of trusting someone and to start connecting deeply with that person instead.

[1.] Interview with the author, Boulder, Colorado, May 6, 1996.

Why do we fear to trust? Because as soon as you let down your guard you allow another person to gain control over your life. If you have sex with someone you give them the power to hurt you as well as to give you pleasure. They may infect you with a sexually transmitted disease, withhold their body, refuse to indulge in your sexual fantasies, or betray you. If you let them know exactly how much money you have, they may pressure you to share it with them. If you expose your emotional vulnerabilities, they may ridicule them or put you down. Or if you share your fears with them, they may use this information to manipulate you. To give away control to someone else is an act of courage.

TRUST TAKES TIME

So how do we ever manage to trust each other sexually or romantically? It doesn't happen in a day. Even when deep intuitive bonding takes place, right from the start you still have to stop, look, and listen. You can't create trust like you make instant coffee. It takes time.

Over a period of weeks, months, and years you test your partner to find out if he is trustworthy. First there are small tests: "Will you stop flirting with that secretary at the office who has an obvious crush on you? It bothers me when you kiss her on the cheek in front of me." Then there are medium-sized tests: "When I work late, will you resist the temptation to go to a bar? If you do, will you go home alone?" And there are big tests: "Will you keep your agreement not to have sex with someone else when you're away on business trips? Will you tell me the truth if you do?" Each time you ask questions like these, trust will either grow or die—depending on how your partner answers them.

The problem with trust is that it's dynamic, not static. People change. Some become more trustworthy, and others become less so. The partner you married who always told you where he was, kept his promise to let you know when he was sexually restless, and shared his erotic fantasies freely may be different now. An addiction, a new philosophy of life, or a change in sexual preference may have moved him in a whole new direction. He may be telling white lies, black lies, or simply ignoring your questions completely. There are no guarantees.

NEGOTIATING TRUST

One way you can measure your partner's trustworthiness is to negotiate—and renegotiate—agreements about controversial sexual or romantic issues. For example, you may both decide not to openly flirt with other people while you are out for the evening together. If your partner repeatedly disregards your agreement, you renegotiate it. Perhaps it's unreasonable to expect both of you not to flirt at all; as long as no overt sexual overtures are made you can both play and tease a bit. If after several renegotiations you partner still keeps breaking agreements, you have a warning: Trust between the two of you is weak. It's a gift; take it as such.

Sometimes you don't find out that your partner is untrustworthy until the stakes are much higher. Andrea, a newspaper reporter, promised Bryan, a supermarket produce manager, that they would live together. She made this promise right after Christmas, and he believed her. But after several overnight visits, she changed her mind and decided that they should keep separate apartments; she realized that she needed her own space. Unfortunately, Andrea waited until Easter before she told Bryan about her change of heart. He was shocked at her betrayal: "I trusted Andrea that our relationship would go in the direction we had agreed upon and it didn't."

The Four Stages of Trust

Trust evolves. We start off as babies with *perfect trust*. Inevitably, trust is *damaged* by our parents or other family members. Depending on the severity, we may experience *devastated trust*, in which the trust is completely broken. In order to heal, we must learn when and how trust can be *restored*. As part of this final step, if we cannot fully trust someone, then we establish guarded, conditional, or selective trust.[2]

PERFECT TRUST

The first people besides ourselves that we learn to trust—or mistrust—are our parents. If they behave with integrity, tell us the truth,

---

[2.] Dee Gritzke, student, conversation with the author, Seattle, Washington, May 14, 1997.

and keep their promises, then we are inclined to believe that other people will do the same thing. If our parents tell us to trust them and then break their word, we may never learn to trust at all.

When Cathy, a college professor, was betrayed, she experienced total mistrust at first. She asked me, "Can I trust anyone: myself, other people, or even God?" I asked her if she remembered feeling this way before. She thought for a moment and then replied, "Yes. When I was a little girl. My father was a minister devoted to spreading the word of God. Yet he beat me and my brother regularly. It seemed so crazy to me. How could someone who was supposed to be so good act so bad? If I couldn't trust him to back up his words with actions, then I couldn't trust anyone else." Since I fully empathized with how Cathy was feeling, it was difficult to disagree with her. But I did tell her that unless she changed her attitude she wouldn't have healthy love relationships in the future.

None of us become adults and retain the perfect trust we were born with. But that doesn't mean we have to go to the opposite extreme. As my good friend author and public speaker Cheewa James puts it, "I trust everybody at the beginning. I assume everyone is loving until proven otherwise."[3] For best results, start off a relationship with the assumption that the other person is trustworthy. Be careful to protect yourself but give him the benefit of the doubt.

DAMAGED TRUST

Inevitably, the person you love will violate your trust. The most common warning signs include:

- *Withholding vital information.* You say, "Where were you last night until 2:00 A.M.?" "Nowhere special."
- *Lying.* He says, "I was working late," but when you called his office, there was no answer.
- *Giving you mixed messages.* He denies your accusations but doesn't look you in the eye.
- *Refusing to negotiate.* When you ask, "Will you promise to stay away from her?" he says, "Leave me alone," and walks away.

---

3. Interview with the author, Sacramento, California, May 10, 1996 (*Catch the Whisper of the Wind*, Deerfield Beach, Florida, Health Communications, Inc., 1995).

Deep in your heart you know that trust has been damaged. When you find out about a betrayal immediately after it happens, trust is broken. But it is not necessarily devastating. Especially if it is a mini-betrayal, you and your partner can talk about the incident, agree that it won't occur again, and reestablish a bond of openness and loyalty.

DEVASTATED TRUST

When your partner violates your limits and behaves in a way you find morally unacceptable, your trust is completely broken. Typically this happens after a betrayal when you've been cheated on, lied to, and treated with profound disrespect.

Devastated trust is a crisis. The first time it happens you may totally regress. You feel as if you're five years old as you reexperience your original fundamental loss. You ask yourself, just as Cathy did, "Whom can I trust?" You may answer your own question, "Not my mother or my father, not even my partner. Who's left?" Before you can think about trusting yourself and other people, you have to deal with the situation at hand. Can trust possibly be restored? If not, you will have to end the relationship despite any remaining good qualities.

What happens if you suddenly find out that you've been betrayed long ago? This happened to Edith, a newspaper editor. After her husband, Joe, returned from a weekend personal growth seminar, he decided to "come clean" about his previous sexual infidelities. Late one night he told Edith that when he had visited an old out-of-town girlfriend five years ago, the two of them had sex. Furthermore, they had both discussed the possibility of ending their marriages so they could have a serious relationship together. "I could never trust Joe again after that," Edith told me. "If he had told me at the time we might have been able to salvage something. But to find out five years later? All this time he'd been withholding vital information. How could I possibly know what else he is hiding now?"

Francesca, a computer technician, was offered a choice. Her husband, George, told her, "During the early years of our marriage I committed a few indiscretions. I'd like to tell you so I can get them off my chest. Is this all right with you?" Francesca thought for a while before she responded, "You can tell me if you like. But if you do I'll never believe another word you say again. The time to tell me was when it happened, not now." Of course, simply by bringing up the subject he shattered her trust completely.

If you suspect that your partner betrayed you, you should confront him as soon as you can. You may rationalize, "I don't want to hurt him, get into an argument, or rock the boat." Short-term pain is long-term gain. Every moment you wait, trust is eroded. Conversely, if you betray your partner either reveal it at the time or else take a vow of eternal silence. Sharing a betrayal farther down the road devastates trust.

If trust is repeatedly broken can it be restored? No. Harriet, a registered nurse, had a tumultuous courtship. Her fiance, Ira, left her to go back to a former girlfriend. When they broke up, he returned to her, promised her an engagement ring, and asked her to marry him. Two weeks later, he spent the weekend with another former girlfriend. Upon his return, he announced that he wanted to postpone their engagement because he wanted to continue dating. Harriet waited patiently until he gave up his second girlfriend. Six months later, she married him. It was a mistake. Harriet said to me, "I actually believed that Ira and I could 'start over.' But it wasn't true. I had lost all respect for him. My trust had been violated so often that I found myself waiting for it to happen again. And Ira continued his habit of having other sexual relationships behind my back. For our relationship to survive it was up to him to take the lead in restoring trust. And he didn't."

RESTORED TRUST

Can you restore sexual or romantic trust once it is damaged or destroyed? It's possible, but difficult. You don't get past a betrayal overnight; it takes months or even years.

The good news is that the aftermath of a betrayal is an opportunity to strengthen your relationship. If you and your partner openly talk about what happened, you will open the gateway to deeper intimacy. While you cannot be positive that you won't be betrayed again you can certainly minimize the chances.

A good exercise for restoring trust is the Trust Meditation found in Appendix A. You can also use it as a model for creating your own personal meditation.

Discuss your partner's motives for betraying you and your own involvement in the cause. Honestly share how you feel and what you need at the present moment. Express your concerns about the future, let each other know what you expect from now on, and state your limits about what you will and won't put up with. If you can't have this kind of conversation by yourselves, then get professional help right away. Don't wait; mistrust can become a habit. A qualified therapist, psychologist, or marriage counselor can guide the two of you as you explore why the betrayal happened and how to prevent another one. Gradually you'll start trusting each other in small matters—and then in bigger ones.

One thing's for sure: You can't turn back the clock. You and your partner don't feel the same way toward each other anymore. Trust has been broken and it's difficult to fix. As you put your relationship back together, both of you see each other differently. You think, "Maybe I can trust this person again but from now on I need to be careful." Your trust is not as complete as it once was. It may be:

- *Guarded trust.* You think, "I'll trust you again, but I'll be on guard for another betrayal. If it happened once it could happen again."
- *Conditional trust.* You think, "I'll trust you again under certain conditions, such as if you never communicate with the accomplice again."
- *Selective trust.* You think, "I'll trust you with money but not with sex. You can continue to write checks on our joint account as you have in the past. But I want detailed information and frequent reassurance that you're being faithful to me."

By making one of these agreements, you take a big first step in the right direction.

But suppose you can't restore trust? What if you feel that you can't trust anyone ever again? Janice, a writer-editor whose trust had been recently devastated, answers: "Since my husband cheated on me I realize that I can be betrayed at any time. In one split second my life can turn upside down. But I don't choose to focus on the uncertainty. If I did, life would be too difficult. I couldn't have a love relationship with anyone So while I'm aware of the danger of trusting other people, I don't obsess. I continue to reach out even though part of me shouts, 'Watch out.'"

Trust and Respect Go Hand in Hand

One reason betrayal is so painful is that it indicates a fundamental lack of respect. I can only betray you if I don't value you, if I don't hold you in high esteem, if I don't honor you, and if I don't consider your feelings as important as mine. After each of my mega-betrayals I asked myself, "Could he do this to me if he really respected and loved me?" Each time the answer was clearly "no." Conversely, you lose respect for someone who betrayed you. That's why it's difficult—if not impossible—to allow yourself to be emotionally vulnerable and to have satisfying sex afterward. You can't be intimate with someone you don't respect.

Two people who trust each other share their nonnegotiable issues. They tell each other what they will and won't put up with. Each will be inclined to respect the other's limits, not because they fear the repercussions of violation but because they are bonded by mutual respect. If they put their feelings into words they would say to each other, "You are very precious to me. I want our relationship to last. I will do my best to be worthy of your trust so you can be relaxed and confident with me." Or, as good friend of mine said to me recently, "Trust me that I will never deliberately do anything that would hurt you, be unloving or be disrespectful."

How You Create Trust

Trust is a choice. While there is no ironclad guarantee that you will *never* be betrayed, you have the power to create trusting romantic and sexual relationships. The moment you meet someone, you can begin to deliberately nurture trust. How?

- *Be in integrity with yourself.* Get in touch with your real needs and feelings so you can disclose them. Know who you are and what you want from a relationship. If you are honest with yourself, you will be honest with other people. If you tell others the truth, they will tend to reciprocate.
- *Select a trustworthy person.* Let your intuition be your guide. If your inner voice gives you a green light, follow it. Observe and listen carefully. If you perceive signs of danger (white lies, black lies, broken promises), heed them. An untrustworthy person isn't going to change overnight even with your good influence.

- *Create trust moment by moment.* Whenever an issue surfaces where you feel your trust is being violated, talk about it. It may make you both uncomfortable in the short run but it will bring you closer together in the long run. If you have serious questions, ask them: "Where were you yesterday evening when I called and got no answer?" "Why were you two hours late for our date tonight?" "Who was that woman who came to your door this morning?" "To whom does this necklace on your dresser belong?" If you feel there's something wrong you're probably right. Always follow your intuition.

To create trust you need to reveal your feelings—both the bad and the good. You need to share the truth about who you are, what's going on for you now, and your intentions for the future. When you notice something that's going on inside you must honestly report it. You must resist the temptation to lie at all costs. Lying kills trust.

If lying is so deadly why do we do it?

- *To look good.* We choose to present an image of ourselves as attractive and desirable. We are afraid to share information that may make us look bad because we think we may lose the person we love. Actually, the opposite is true. Intimacy begins when you stop pretending to be perfect and start being real with your partner.
- *To avoid unpleasantness.* We conceal information that we believe may cause conflict. We want our love to last so we go to great lengths to create false, superficial harmony. This is another self-destructive myth. As Dr. Judith Sherven and Dr. James Sniechowski point out, we get to know each other better as we reveal and negotiate our differences.[4]
- *To avoid hurting our partner's feelings.* We don't want to upset our partner by saying something that might make him angry. We want to protect him from upset. This is another self-destructive

---

[4.] Judith Sherven and James Sniechowski, *The New Intimacy: Finding the Passion at the Heart of Your Differences.* Deerfield Beach, Florida, Health Communications, Inc., 1997.

strategy. Yes, you may cause an upset by saying something your partner may find offensive, but sometimes you have to air your negative feelings to get an honest, positive dialogue going.

In *Radical Honesty* Dr. Brad Blanton recommends that couples share their complete sexual histories with each other.[5] I agree. The more honest information you have about your partner's sexual preferences, habits, and style, the easier it is to satisfy him. And to protect yourself. For example, if your partner is uncomfortable with monogamy—and you know it—you can agree to go your separate ways or else to use condoms to protect yourselves from disease.

THE SECRET OF CREATING TRUST

A friend of mine posed this question to me: "If I tell you the truth— that I lied to you—can you still trust me?" Clearly the answer is "yes." The secret of creating trust right from the beginning is to have a conversation that goes something like this, "I have betrayed other people. I may betray you sometimes and you will probably betray me. We will try to avoid it, but when it happens we will deal with it together."

I have been in relationships with people who proved untrustworthy. They could have spared me—and themselves—a lot of grief by being honest about their untrustworthiness. They might have said to me, "Sometimes I tell white lies; often I tell black ones. I might even sleep with someone else and not tell you about it. Do you want to have sex and romance with me on these terms?" If I had answered "yes," I would have gone into the relationship with my eyes open. At least I would have had a choice.

Similarly, people who want an extramarital affair can clear the air by being honest with their accomplice and with their partner about their intentions. When an attractive married man invites me to have sex with him, I reply, "Go tell your wife. If it's okay with her it's all right with me." Most of them reply, "If I tell her she'll kick me out." My answer is, "At least she'll know what you're up to. Then the two of you can make a decision about what to do next."

[5.] Brad Blanton, *Radical Honesty*, New York, Dell Publishing, 1996.

Personally, I believe that ongoing and complete sexual disclosure is the most powerful building block of trust. Granted, you have to be a very secure person in a very strong relationship—and very few of us are—to share your complete sexual self with your partner. But if you can manage, it works. For example, a married colleague of mine had extra-marital sex without intercourse with another woman while we were attending a convention. He insisted on calling his wife (who was at home taking care of their children) and telling her the details. Naturally she was furious. When I spoke to him a couple of weeks later he reported that they had a huge argument, cleared the air, and decided that she had equal rights to sexual pleasure with other men (and that they would hire a babysitter).

Other people take an even more radical position. I recently received a letter from a former judge which posed this question: "If you know your partner is going to have sex with other people would you rather he did it behind your back or with your knowledge? Or would you prefer that he was miserable repressing his desires?" Then he answered his own question, "Of course you'd rather have a satisfied partner and know what's going on."

Complete sexual honesty is the antidote to betrayal. You and your partner can share your fantasies and your experience. It may be painful, but it's also liberating. Your emotional intimacy will skyrocket. In the long run, you will feel infinitely more relaxed. You will no longer be afraid of being betrayed.

Chapter 9

Feel Sexually Safe Again

efore you can trust someone you must feel physically safe. This is the most fundamental ingredient of trust. Women especially feel vulnerable when we first meet someone. If we haven't had our own bodies misused, abused, or assaulted, don't we know someone else who has? We best reveal our emotions and unleash our sexuality when we are confident we will not be hurt.

Sexual betrayal makes you feel physically vulnerable. You think, "What is my betrayer going to do to me next? Anything's possible." You don't feel respected; you don't feel valued. Sex loses its joy. There is a spiritual letdown, an emotional distancing. You lie in bed next to him night after night longing to have sex but somehow you can't open up. The two of you may not be able to connect sexually at all. This is healthy. If you continue to have sex with your betrayer, it can be extremely destructive. Since you feel endangered during lovemaking, you do whatever you have to do to protect your inner self. You go through the motions of sex but hold back the passion. Your body splits off from your spirit and your emotions. Frequently you find yourself fantasizing about someone else when you are aroused. You use this strategy to distance yourself.

It takes at least six months to restore sexual trust—to reunite your body with your feelings and your soul. During this time you may be sorely tempted to rush out and find another romantic partner right away. Or you may feel like being sexually promiscuous and seek multiple short-term relationships. Neither of these behaviors will benefit you over the long term. To feel sexually safe again you need to go within, release the pain you've experienced, and prepare yourself to trust again. If you cannot do this alone, consult a qualified sex therapist.

One-Night Stands

What about one-night stands? Yes, they can enable you to reconnect with your sexuality for a brief period of time. But the morning-after hangover can be agonizing. If you haven't taken proper precautions, you put yourself in mortal danger. Instead of worrying about losing your sex drive you are now concerned about losing your life. Even if you did use protection, chances are you will never see the other person again. What an emotionally devastating experience!

If you must be promiscuous:

- *Practice safe sex.* Always use a condom when you're having intercourse.
- *Be straightforward about your intentions.* Let the other person know you are looking for a brief encounter and not a long-term, committed relationship.
- *Take the time to find out where your playmate is at.* Select someone who is also out for a good time and nothing more.

When You Feel Sexually Blocked

You attract people on your level of sexual and emotional development. If you do your own inner work before you seek another partner, you will minimize your chances of another violation of trust.

After a betrayal, you are gifted with a unique opportunity to explore yourself sexually. Ask yourself these questions:

- *Which types of sexual experiences give me the most pleasure?* (intercourse, foreplay without intercourse, fantasy)
- *What sex acts do I enjoy most?* (oral sex, genital sex, intercourse)
- *What kinds of sexual experiences have I been having that I want to avoid in the future ?* (boring, routine sex; sex where my needs didn't count; infrequent, passionless sex)
- *What kind of new sexual experiences do I crave?* (having sex at new locations, such as the beach or a luxury hotel room; being sexual at different times of day, such as in the morning; exploring sexual fantasies with phonesex, cybersex, videosex, or sex toys; experiencing sex with more than one person)

- *What sexual style do I prefer?* (hard or soft touch; slow or fast rhythm; nakedness or sexy clothing: lots of foreplay or hardly any at all; music, candles, incense, and dim lighting or no particular romantic ambiance; explicit sexual language or lack of it; lots of communicating or being sexual in silence)
- *Can I comfortably share these sexual preferences with someone else?* (or am I embarrassed to discuss them? Would I prefer to find out by trial and error instead?)
- *Can I ask a prospective partner about his tastes?* (and am I able to listen carefully to whatever he replies?)

Your answers to these questions can guide you in your search for an appropriate partner.

No matter who your next partner is, he is not in charge of making sex enjoyable for you. *You are responsible for your own sexual satisfaction.* You can learn to control and release your own sexual energy so you can have orgasms at will. You can learn to arouse yourself during foreplay and intercourse rather than relying entirely on someone else to stimulate you. Many women and most men can learn how to have multiple orgasms.[1]

To get ready for your next sex partner start by having sex with yourself. For one thing, self-stimulation is safe. For another thing, it's an opportunity to explore your own sexuality. Masturbating to please yourself instead of with the goal of pleasing another person is a totally different experience. You're not trying to get yourself aroused in preparation for sex or to release excess sexual energy afterward. Many people feel more sexually safe alone than with someone else.

Another way to learn more about your own sexuality is to explore your sexual fantasies. Become a "sexual spectator" instead of a participant. Get out some books on sex from the library, buy a couple of sexually oriented magazines, or rent a few sexually explicit videotapes. Try

---

[1] For more information about how to achieve multiple orgasm, I recommend this tape and guidebook for men: Jack Johnson, M.A., *Male Multiple Orgasm,* 1257 Siskiyou Boulevard, #195-B, Ashland, Oregon, Jack Johnson Seminars, 1995. For women I suggest Avodah K. Offit, *Night Thoughts: Reflections of a Sex Therapist,* Northvale, New Jersey, Jason Aronson, Inc., 1995, pp. 25–41.

a phonesex chat line or visit several sexually oriented computer Web sites. Ask yourself, "What kinds of sex appeal to me? What would I like to do that I've never tried before?" When you're feeling even more bold consider new options. Ask yourself, "Might I enjoy the swinger lifestyle? Would it be fun to try being part of a threesome?"

I strongly recommend that you abstain from sex with a partner for six months to a year after a mega-betrayal. Why? First, because you allow yourself time to let the bad memories fade. Second, because you give yourself the space for your new sexual self to emerge. Third, because you enable yourself to ask these pertinent questions: *"What went wrong? How can I have a satisfying sexual relationship in the future?"* Otherwise, you'll keep on replaying the same scenario of betrayal over and over again.

SELECT YOUR NEXT PARTNER CAREFULLY

Another sexual betrayal while you are still vulnerable can devastate you. Sex without trust is abusive. You need someone with whom you feel safe both sexually and emotionally.

Check out each person you meet carefully. Don't rush into a sexual relationship right away—ask pertinent questions, such as, "Are you married? Are you monogamous? Are you HIV positive? Are you bisexual? Are you gay? Are you honest about having sex with other people? Have you recently been sexually betrayed? Do you frequently betray others?" Don't be shy. You seek a partner who fits your unique needs and preferences. You are avoiding a "double whammy" by screening beforehand.

Your new partner shouldn't be a carbon copy of your betrayer. You don't want to repeat your old mistakes. In fact, you'd prefer someone very different, even though it takes a while to get used to a new sexual style. You definitely seek a person who is going to tell you the truth about his sexuality. Ideally, the two of you will be sexually compatible. With honesty and mutual sexual satisfaction, you will minimize the chances of another betrayal.

ESTABLISH TRUST BEFORE YOU HAVE SEX

Before you have sex again, you must firmly establish sexual trust. Even if an attractive prospective partner comes on to you like gangbusters, don't get sexual right away. An initially exciting sexual connection will keep you from seeing the other person as he really is. Do whatever it takes to resist the temptation to jump into bed if you don't feel right. Talk on the phone, meet for lunch, or write letters to each other until you are confident that you are being treated with honesty and respect.

Why? Because if there is no sexual trust, you'll panic the morning after. Your mind will go crazy with thoughts like these: "Why didn't he call? Did it mean anything to him? Is he out having sex with someone else? Do I expect a commitment of exclusivity? Does he?" If you discuss these issues openly *before* you have sex, you'll feel a lot more relaxed afterward. You certainly don't want to be betrayed again.

The "Three Ts" of Sexual Trust

You don't get over a sexual betrayal overnight. Renewing sexual trust is a long, slow process. Initially you spend several months doing your own sexual inventory. You go within to learn more about your sexual self so you can connect with a compatible partner. Then you devote time and energy to finding someone who is honest, respectful, and trustworthy. Once you have found a suitable prospective partner you begin to build trust together. Both of you will:

1. *Talk to each other.*
2. *Touch each other.*
3. *Take time to let trust grow.*

TALK TO EACH OTHER

It's a trite phrase, but it's true: Be friends first. Get to know each other. Ask your prospective sexual partner if he's been betrayed recently and listen to his story. Tell your partner about your betrayal—not *ad nauseam,* but enough so he knows where you're coming from. Talk about how you want your sexual relationships to be different this time.

Slowly start becoming emotionally intimate. Report what you notice about yourself and your partner in the present moment. Little by little share your vulnerabilities, faults, and imperfections. Stop trying to look good and start being real.

Share your sexual self openly and honestly. You want someone you can count on to care for you as a human being, not as a sexual object. Describe your past sexual experiences, your present fears, and your future intentions.

Also insist upon full and honest disclosure from your partner of his sexual history, sexual concerns, and current sexual activities. You're not interrogating him, but you want to know the truth. No more surprises!

TOUCH EACH OTHER

Once you've spent time talking and listening to each other, you're ready to start touching—gently, slowly, and noninvasively. You want to feel relaxed as you surrender to a profound feeling of trust. You don't want to feel attacked or else your reflexes will propel you to defend yourself.

Nonsexual touch comes first. You may wish to try the following exercise as a model, or choose a different method of getting comfortable together. Put a piece of quiet music on. Start by lying next to each other in bed or on a rug and breathing together in unison: in, out; in, out; in out. Notice which parts of your body are tense and focus on loosening them up. Now try meditating together: Be in silence for a few moments, repeating a phrase or word over and over to yourself to quiet your mind. If you feel relaxed, close your eyes and go to sleep. It's a real test of sexual trust when you awaken and feel safe. Afterward, take time to discuss what you have experienced—or whatever else comes up for you.

When both of you feel comfortable with nonsexual touching, you're ready to move toward becoming sexual. Go back to your bed or your rug and start snuggling. Better yet, give each other a massage. (If you don't know how, buy or borrow a book that will teach you.[2]) If you prefer to be touched softly or firmly, say so. If there are certain body parts you would prefer your partner stayed away from, let him know. If you don't like to be tickled, speak up. Your intention is to feel relaxed with each other, not to be nervous about what will happen next.

[2.] The best book I know with simple, easy-to-follow instructions about how to give your lover a massage is George Downing's *The Massage Book*, illustrated by Anne Kent Rush, New York, Random House, 1984. (This book has been reprinted at least twenty-six times, so it should be easy to locate a copy.)

Sometimes it helps if your partner tells you in advance what he's going to do: "Now I'm going to move my hands upward and softly touch your face." After you're comfortable with nonsexual touch, holding hands and kissing are tried-and-true ways to show affection—and to move toward the erotic.

Watch out for signs that you have entered a danger zone. If at any point you feel uncomfortable, let your partner know immediately. You may be triggering memories of your recent betrayal. These must be addressed to reestablish sexual trust. In her tape "Love Trauma," Dr. Judith Swack tells the story of a woman who had, as she puts it, "a sexual history from hell." After she had sex with a new partner, she got a flashback from one of her earlier traumas. The woman sat bolt upright in bed; said, "Excuse me"; and proceeded to use the Callahan Method to release her fear. When she finished, the two of them snuggled up together and laughed.[3] If you and your partner learn Dr. Swack's excellent techniques, you can use them to deal with your sexual fears (and his) whenever they appear.

When you consistently experience strong physical trust you are ready to have sex. How do you know? You feel in control, that your needs are being respected, and that you are safe. It is still possible that from time to time you will feel attacked when memories of your past betrayal are inadvertently triggered. You and your partner can agree upon signals that you will give each other to say, "Stop; I'm not ready for this." You will promise each other to honor them so neither of you will shut down sexually.

It's best to communicate your sexual likes and dislikes before you actually have sex. Now is the time you will reap the benefits of learning about yourself during your recent period of sexual solitude. "No, thank you, I don't indulge in anal sex. It's dangerous." Or "Yes, I would love to experiment with new sexual positions during intercourse." If you aren't comfortable with words, then use gestures while you are being sexual. Say no by tightening your legs or turning away; say, yes by guiding your partner's body or moving his hand where you want it to go.

[3.] Judith Swack, Ph.D., *Love Trauma*, Needham, Massachusetts, Judith Swack and Associates, 1997.

IT TAKES TIME TO FEEL SEXUALLY SAFE

Don't rush. It may take months or even years before you experience sexual trust again. It's worth waiting for. Sex is best when both of you are totally comfortable with each other. Only then will your sex drive return to normal.

If you find that your prospective partner does not support you in your quest for sexual trust, it is time to move on. Keep looking until you find someone who will. Remember, don't be swayed by superficialities. What you want is not the tall, dark, handsome stranger you've been fantasizing about. You are in search of a loving, caring, sensitive human being who *listens to what you have to say, respects your wishes,* and above all, *is patient with you.* This can either be a new lover or your betrayer if you decide to take him back.

Chapter 10

Should You Take Him Back?

*Y*ou've conquered your pain, rebuilt your life, and begun to trust again. But you haven't yet answered the most difficult question, "Should you take your betrayer back?" There's no simple answer because everyone's situation is different.

Four Typical Dilemmas

I find betrayed people everywhere. While in the checkout line at a Chicago supermarket I say hello to Leonard. As he carries my groceries out to my car he starts to cry. When I ask him, "What's the matter?" he puts down the bags, sits down on the sidewalk, and weeps. Finally he manages to tell me: "My girlfriend's been sleeping with someone else. I just found out last weekend. Should I take her back? I love her more than words. She says she still loves me, too and she's sorry for what she did. Will you please pray that I make the right decision?" *What should Leonard do?*

Marianne, a sculptor, tells me a different story. "My husband Nick and I were married for ten years and even had a child together before I found out he was gay. I had been dissatisfied with the infrequency of our sex for the past several years, but Nick insisted I was "oversexed" and I believed him. Now he says he wants to move out and live with his male lover. He'll take the children on weekends and they'll be better off. He insists there's no point in continuing our relationship; he's never desired me sexually so it's all been a sham. But I still care for him and am trying to convince him to go with me to therapy. Maybe we can work out an arrangement in which he'll stay with me and the kids and also see his lover from time to time. At least I'll know what's going on." *What should Marianne do?*

Everyone has her or his own special dilemma. Consider Phyllis and Ron. They had been married for eighteen years and have two handsome teenage sons. Phyllis is a pharmacist who has devoted herself to her family since her first son was born. Ron is a successful company president who has just turned fifty. During a midlife crisis he decided that there's more to life than being a husband and father. He secretly began an affair with his blonde, attractive, twenty-three-year-old secretary, Natalie. One day he confessed his infidelity to Phyllis and told her he was moving out to live with Natalie. He said he feels younger and more alive when they're together. Ron packed a suitcase but left all his other possessions behind.

Six weeks later Phyllis called Oscar, a close male friend, to tell him what happened. "I'll be right over," Oscar replied. He had been in love with Phyllis for several years; he was delighted because an opportunity for them to be together had finally appeared. Oscar started visiting Phyllis regularly. She enjoyed his company; unlike Ron he's warmhearted, funny, and an excellent listener. Phyllis and Oscar started having sex together. In the meantime Ron came by regularly to visit the children. One evening he told Phyllis he would like to move back home. Phyllis asked him if he was willing to stop seeing Natalie. Ron replied "I'm not sure. What happens if I give her up and then you kick me out? Then I'll have no one. Are you willing to stop seeing Oscar and be faithful to me?" *What should Phyllis do?*

Then there's Tim and Ursula. They have been married for ten years and have a five-year-old girl and a seven-year-old boy. Ursula is a commercial artist and Tim is a laboratory scientist. Bored with his marriage and his job, Tim started secretly going out for drinks with Sheila, a colleague of his, after work. After a few weeks, they rented a hotel room and had sex. For the first time in many years Tim felt fully alive; sex with Sheila was much more exciting than anything he had ever experienced with Ursula.

After Tim started coming home late several evenings a week, Ursula confronted him. "Yes, I've been sleeping with Sheila," he admitted. "But I'm not ready to leave you yet." Ursula began to weep. She said, "How do you expect us to go on like this? It tortures me to live with you while you're making love with someone else. And it's bad for the children that you're away from home so much now. What are we going to tell them? They already sense that something is wrong. " *What should Ursula do?*

How Do You Feel?

Typically there are two different sets of feelings after a betrayal. Which one is yours?

- I still love you and I want you to stay. It's impossible to forget but I will try to forgive. I realize that you may betray me again and I will protect myself.
- This betrayal is driving me crazy. I won't allow myself to be abused by you anymore. I want to end this relationship, be by myself, or find someone new.

At first you may experience both kinds of emotions alternately. In the morning you wake up thinking, "I want him to stay," but by afternoon you say to yourself, "I want to end this relationship." Eventually one set of feelings will prevail.

FIFTEEN QUESTIONS TO ASK YOURSELF

But what if you want to decide right now? Does a mega-betrayal—or several mini-betrayals—mean your relationship is over? To help make up your mind, ask yourself these fifteen questions:

1. *Is this the first time I have been betrayed by this person?* Or is it one of a long series of betrayals that have taken place over the years? Is another one likely to happen? Or are there unusual circumstances that have provoked this particular betrayal?
2. *Is my betrayer genuinely sorry?* How has he demonstrated his repentance? With words or with actions? Has he stated his intention to behave differently in the future? Once, or more than once?
3. *Is my betrayer willing to make amends?* If so, specifically how is he going to make up to me for all the pain I've been through? Is what he offers to do what I need? Is it enough to satisfy me?
4. *Is my betrayer willing to give up his relationship with the accomplice?* Partly or completely? Do I trust my betrayer to follow through on this promise? What evidence do I have that the two of them won't continue to see each other?
5. *Does my betrayer genuinely want to stay with me?* Short-term or long-term? Is he willing to work together with me to preserve our relationship? Has it lasted at least ten years already?

Does my betrayer still love me? How has he demonstrated his affection since the betrayal?

6. *Does my betrayer intend to show me integrity, loyalty, and honesty in the future?* How has he indicated his intention? Has trust been damaged or is it completely devastated? Can it be restored?

7. *Is my betrayer willing to reexamine our relationship?* Has he already started to do so? Are we already in conversation about what went wrong? Are we brainstorming together what we are going to do differently in the future? How much progress have we made?

8. *Has my betrayer agreed to go to therapy or a support group?* Do we agree on a specific therapist or group? Have we budgeted the time and money? Have we begun to go or when will we start?

9. *Am I still in love with my betrayer?* Or are we hanging on by force of habit? Do I miss my betrayer? Am I starting to feel romantic interest toward other people? Do I visualize myself continuing my relationship with my betrayer or starting over with someone else?

10. *Do I still respect my betrayer?* Does he respect me? How have we recently shown that we value, honor, and cherish each other? Are we going to continue this practice?

11. *Can I ever feel safe again?* Has there been physical violence or emotional abuse? Am I afraid that it will continue? What do I have to do to protect myself in the future? Am I comfortable living under these circumstances?

12. *Am I still having sex with my betrayer?* How often? Do I have an orgasm? Is sex with my betrayer becoming better or less pleasurable for me each time? Have we considered sex therapy?

13. *Am I able to begin to forgive my betrayer?* How strong are my feelings of anger and disappointment? Are they increasing or decreasing as time passes? Can I express them without further damaging our relationship?

14. *Is there enough joy when we're together to outweigh the pain I'm going through?* Have we recently shared some happy moments? Do I expect to have more?

15. (If there are children) *Would our children be better off if we stayed together?* Are they now having problems at home or at school? Can we arrange for them to have regular access to both parents if we go our separate ways?

The last question is open to debate. Do children grow up healthier in a two-parent home or in a single-parent one? Many people believe that a home in which both mother and father live together is better for children no matter how the parents get along. Others, myself included, think that it's better for children to grow up in a harmonious home atmosphere with one happy parent than to live with constant fighting or to witness "sneaking around." It's up to you to decide.

FIVE QUESTIONS TO IGNORE

Please note the five questions you should *not* ask yourself:

1. *What will my family and friends think?* It doesn't matter as long as you are comfortable with your decision. They'll get used to it.
2. *Would it look better professionally or socially to preserve the relationship?* You are not putting on a show. This is your life. Social or professional prestige is far less important than your personal happiness.
3. *Is it more convenient to stay together?* Force of habit isn't a good enough excuse to stay together. Yes, you'll have to make changes in your lifestyle, but at least you'll have your integrity. Do you want to live with someone who continues to deceive you?
4. *Can I make it financially if I am alone?* It may be a struggle in the short run, but it will be well worth it in the long run. Wouldn't you rather wear second-hand clothes than be treated with profound disrespect? Wouldn't you prefer to do all the household chores by yourself for a while instead of being haunted by a partner who is dishonest with you?
5. *Do I want to give up readily available sex even though it's not optimal?* It may be difficult at first to find another sex partner, but the sex will most likely be much better the next time around. Why not try having sex with yourself for a while?

Four Dilemmas Resolved

Remember Leonard, Marianne, Phyllis, and Ursula? As I guided them through their confusion, we found answers that were right for them.

1. *What should Leonard do?* When I asked Leonard the appropriate questions, he replied, "Yes, it's the first time. She says she is going to make it up to me in a thousand ways. She wants to stay with me and promises that she'll never go to bed with him again." I advised him to take her back and give her one more chance.

2. *What about Marianne?* During our conversation she revealed, "I'm not sure Nick has ever really loved me. I think he married to convince his friends and family he was heterosexual. I'm not even sure if this is his first affair; he may have had other male lovers that he never told me about. He refuses to get counseling or even to talk to me about our problems. I love him and I'm willing to forgive him, but it takes two to make a marriage work." I told Marianne that she should release Nick and go on with her life.

3. *What decision should Phyllis make?* Ron's never betrayed me before," she told me. "He's been faithful and honest since the day we met. Turning fifty and reaching the top of the ladder of success just turned his head. I do forgive him for what he did. I won't let him move back home until he promises to give up Natalie, but he and I are talking about our problems. We even started going to therapy together last week.

   "It's true, I care deeply for Oscar, but Ron is the father of my children and that makes a huge difference to me. Oscar and I have great sex and lots of fun, but Ron and I have a special kind of respect for each other because we've struggled and raised a family together. So I'm open to the possibility of his returning home. " I agreed with Phyllis. She should take Ron back once he ends his affair. She won't ever completely forget what happened, but she *can* choose to let go of the past and live in the present.

4. *What's the right course of action for Ursula?* She told me sadly, "Tim cheated on me even before we got married. I should have ended our relationship a long time ago. Even though I've begged him, he refuses to stop having sex with Sheila and continues to

come home late during the week. He's even started sneaking out of the house on weekends. When I ask Tim to tell me what's wrong, he says, 'There's nothing to talk about.' He's in therapy by himself right now, but he refuses to go to marriage counseling with me." I told Ursula that she should not take him back unless he ends his relationship with Sheila. "Stop pleading with him and start separation proceedings," I advised.

If You Stay in Your Relationship

If you decide to take your betrayer back, be prepared to be flexible and understanding. One step forward, two steps back is how progress is made at the beginning. Although you are committed to giving the relationship one more try, you must realize that your betrayer may violate your trust at any time. So protect yourself financially, emotionally, and sexually. Make sure you're earning your own living. Extend your circle of friends. Use a condom while having intercourse if you suspect your betrayer of another infidelity.

If You Leave Your Betrayer

If you still don't know what to do, be assured that in time the answer will become clear. If the emotional abuse increases, if the assault on your self-esteem becomes too devastating, get out. Your life's too precious to waste. Eventually you *will* find someone who will treat you better.

Once you have made the decision not to take your betrayer back, you have some serious work to do on yourself. Don't expect to go "cold turkey" right away; you may be able to arrange a physical separation but it will take a while to distance yourself emotionally and sexually.[1] Here's how you know when you've succeeded. You stop:

- Calling your betrayer just to say hello
- Finding excuses to get together
- Getting into petty arguments about details that used to bother you
- Having sexual fantasies about him
- Feeling jealous of the accomplice

[1] For a detailed discussion of how to separate from a partner read Diane Vaughan, *Uncoupling: Turning Points in Intimate Relationships*, New York, Vintage Books, 1990.

Instead, you channel your energy toward your own personal growth. You start:

- Redesigning your living space
- Giving yourself a make-over
- Thinking about changing jobs or careers
- Developing new interests
- Going new places
- Making new friends

You start thinking different thoughts, focusing on yourself instead of your betrayer. Instead of being depressed, you feel optimistic. As Ivan Burnell, personal growth seminar leader and author of *Say Yes to Life*, puts it, "You say to yourself, 'The path I have followed has been destroyed. The universe is telling me to follow another. I will embrace it. I will leave the room I've been stuck in and close the door behind me. I can go into the hallway to open new doors only after I've shut the old one tight.'"[2]

DON'T BE A "WALKING WOUNDED"

Whether or not you decide to take your betrayer back, you must not let the betrayal run you. Don't be a "walking wounded," a person who constantly lives in fear of another bad experience. After Vinny got divorced, he reconnected with Yvonne, his former high school sweetheart. They had sex and dated for three months, but they did not make a commitment to each other. One evening Yvonne suddenly announced that she's going to marry a former boyfriend of hers. Vinny was devastated by her betrayal. For the next five years he didn't date or have sex with anyone. He was alone—and lonely. To find happiness in love, he had to risk trusting someone else again.

Yes, from time to time you may relapse into mistrust, fear, anguish, and doubt. But as the old proverb says, "Get back on the horse after you fall off or you'll never learn to ride." Trust, love, joy, and faith are out there waiting for you to embrace them. You *can* turn the tables on your betrayer. The aftermath of your betrayal can be tragedy—or a life well-lived.

---

2. Interview with the author, June 9, 1996 (*Say Yes to Life*, I.P.D. Publishing, Center Ossipee, New Hampshire, 1997).

Chapter 11

Turn the Tables on the Betrayer

*Y*ou are about to read the most important chapter in this book. It's about forgiveness. I'm not referring to the conventional meaning of the word: "I'm good; you're bad. I'm doing *you* a big favor by forgiving you for the terrible thing you did. I'm going to forget all about it even though it practically destroyed me." I'm talking about a different kind of forgiveness. "We're both imperfect humans. My forgiving you benefits *me*. Although I'll never forget how you hurt me, I don't choose to dwell on the past."[1]

When you forgive someone in this sense you come from a position of humility, not arrogance. You look inward and realize your own fallibility. How can you condemn your betrayer when you have your own weaknesses and faults? You say to yourself, "There but for the grace of God go I. If I were in your position I might have done the same thing." You refuse to allow your bitterness to blind you to the good qualities of your betrayer. (After all, you initially selected him as a sexual partner.) You realize that if you continue to obsess over the betrayal and allow your resentment to simmer, *you* are the one who will wind up with an ulcer. When you refuse to forgive someone else, you betray yourself.[2]

Forgiveness, in this sense, is a miracle. The moment it begins you start to heal. As it grows you move toward a place of wholeness. You realize that what happened was a gift from the Universe. You weren't on the right path. You were stuck in an unloving, passionless relationship;

[1.] For an excellent discussion of forgiveness in relationships see John Gray, *What Your Mother Couldn't Tell You and Your Father Didn't Know*, New York, HarperCollins, 1994, pp. 420–25.

[2.] The best way I know to start forgiving is to read *A Course in Miracles*®, especially Lesson 68, p. 116.

now that your direction has shifted, you have an opportunity to experience real joy—perhaps for the first time. If you and your betrayer are hoping to forgive each other and remain together, you may wish to use the Forgiveness Meditation found in Appendix B. As always, you may also wish to create your own meditation, using mine as an example.

How to Forgive

IF YOU'VE BEEN BETRAYED

Up to now I've shared with you a lot of material that I trust you are finding useful. Now I want to write you a personal letter. Please read it as if it had your name on it; change the details so that they apply to your unique situation. My purpose is to end your nightmare of betrayal and allow you to finally be at peace with yourself.

> Dear Betrayed:
> Right now you are feeling the agony of betrayal. I empathize with all the pain, rage, and fear that you feel. Rest assured these feelings will disappear—if you allow them to.
> The miracle that heals betrayal is forgiveness. To err is human, to forgive is divine. Jesus was the quintessential betrayed person. His words on the cross, "Forgive them Lord, they know not what they do," had inspired billions of people. Let it inspire you.
> Your betrayer has hurt you badly. Invite him to make it up to you. Perhaps you have a lawyer, priest, minister, rabbi, friend, or relative to back you up. Perhaps you don't. In either case, you have to be your own advocate. Stand up for yourself. Don't let the betrayer get away with it. He has to learn that betrayal has painful consequences.
> Receiving reparations is a healthy way to heal. Take your anger and turn it into righteous indignation. Ask for what you need—and believe you're entitled to get it. Perhaps it's tangible amends: a gift of money or property, a vacation, or help around the

house. Perhaps it's intangible amends: emotional support or a shared spiritual experience such as meditating or going to church together. It might be just spending a couple of hours together being completely honest with each other.

I pray for your healing. Please write to me in care of my publisher, Adams Media Corporation, and tell me how you conquered your pain, rebuilt your life, and restored sexual trust. Sharing your story with me—and with others—will accelerate your progress.

Blessings,
RIKI

IF YOU'RE A BETRAYER

Up to now I've been talking only to readers who have been betrayed. I still have much of value to share with them. But I also want to directly address people reading this book who are betrayers or accomplices. It hasn't been easy for them either. They have their own issues. Perhaps they're in an untenable position right now and don't know how to extricate themselves.

If you're a betrayer, this next letter is for you. Pretend your partner has composed it. You may change the details so that it applies to your special situation.

Dear Betrayer:

At this point there is no way you can turn back the clock. The pain you have caused me can never be erased. The real question is, How are you going to make it up to me now? At the very least you can show me how sorry you are both with words and with actions.

Saying, "I apologize" helps a lot. Even more important is to make amends to me with deeds. I'm going to tell you exactly what I need and I trust that you will do it. Rather than making demands I am giving you a precious gift: an opportunity to demonstrate your integrity. By behaving in a trustworthy

BETRAYED!
∽∾

manner—and keeping the promises you make—you can restore a modicum of trust to our relationship.

Deep inside you are a good person. I don't believe you deliberately intended to be malicious or cruel to me. You found yourself in an impossible situation. Our relationship had problems you couldn't talk about. Driven by unquenchable passion you broke away from me to seek sexual and romantic fulfillment elsewhere. It took a lot of courage for you to confront me and to confess what you had done.

I forgive you. When I am ready I will decide whether to stay with you or to distance myself and find someone new. In the meantime—and always—I wish you well.

Love,
BETRAYED

IF YOU'RE AN ACCOMPLICE

If you're an accomplice, please read this letter. Imagine that your betrayer's partner has written it directly to you.

Dear Accomplice:

I am writing this letter to you in a spirit of compassion. In similar circumstances I might also be tempted just as you were. You were lonely. You met someone irresistibly attractive. He told you how miserable he was and how happy you could make him. Perhaps you knew he was already in a committed relationship; perhaps you didn't. One thing led to another. You formed a friendship, you had sex, you fell in love. Now you want this person—who happens in fact to be in a committed relationship with me—to commit to you.

Yes, I'm angry at you for allowing the betrayal to happen. I envy the fun, the sex, and the intimacy the two of you have. I'm hurting because what has been taken away from me has been given to you.

You see, you did have a choice. You could have kept on asking questions until you found out the truth. When you discovered that your prospective partner was unavailable you could have taken a firm stand. "No, I will not get romantically or sexually involved with you until you have left your partner." This would have been the right thing to do. He, you, and I would have had peace of mind. We would have had respect for ourselves and each other. We would have had a chance to preserve our relationship and you would be free to find someone who was available.

I forgive you. At the same time I admit that I fantasize that you will be betrayed—by the very same person who betrayed me. Only then will you understand what I've been through. But I'm not going to waste any more of my time in futile imaginings. Let's all get on with our lives.

Sincerely,
BETRAYED

SHOW COMPASSION

If you had not been an accomplice, you and "Betrayed" might have become friends. Given the circumstances, now it's best that you never meet. If by some remote chance you do run into each other, allow "Betrayed" to express her feelings, whatever they are. Just imagine how you'd feel if you were in her place.

Similarly, if your new partner tells you that he needs to spend a lot of time at home before he exits, understand. The two of you will be together for a long time to come. Zoe, a cocktail waitress, couldn't wait. She was so impatient to be with her new lover that she moved to his city even before he'd left home. His wife was understandably furious, and it took more time for her to forgive the two of them.

How to Turn the Tables on Betrayal

Forgiveness rewrites the script of betrayal. Once you forgive, you gain control of the situation. Instead of being a victim, you regain your power. Instead of obsessing over the accomplice, you forget all about her. Instead of hurting yourself, you embark on a path of healing.

Betrayal can actually lead to a better romantic relationship—and a stronger you. Perhaps you have decided to take back your betrayer. You conclude: "What happened was an isolated incident, my betrayer is an otherwise trustworthy person, and I can get past this betrayal." Consequently you have renewed confidence in him and in yourself. You can move from fear to love and restore trust.

Or perhaps you have decided not to take your betrayer back; you want to move on. You believe that you have done the right thing and stand firm in your convictions. You have the courage to begin another relationship and to risk another betrayal. You start asking probing questions—and giving honest answers. Slowly you learn to trust again.

Your prescription for your next relationship is:

- *No keeping big secrets (but you still maintain your privacy)*
- *No telling lies*
- *No hiding deep feelings*
- *No living in fear of another betrayal*

It all starts with forgiveness. Once you take this crucial step you move away from fear back to love. You stop judging your betrayer and start empathizing with him instead. You let go of the past and live in the present. Your energy is positive, loving, and nurturing.

How do you know when you've finally reached this sacred place? You feel at peace within. You can say these words and mean them:

I forgive my betrayer and the accomplice.
I forgive myself.
I love myself.
I trust the Universe.

At the same time, you always remain vigilant. You protect yourself in your romantic and sexual relationships—whether you remain with your betrayer or start again with someone new.

Chapter 12

The End of Innocence

$\mathcal{U}$p to now you may have thought betrayal could never happen to you. Now you know it can. Your innocence is over. "If betrayal is an inevitable fact of life, how can I possibly enter into another relationship?" you wonder.

Navigating the "Danger Zone"

Yes, it's difficult. When you trust again you become vulnerable. Every time you express your sexual desire you risk rejection. Whenever you emotionally bond you risk betrayal. *Welcome to the danger zone.* You have moved from love to fear. You realize that at any time you may be abused, devalued, or abandoned again. You are stressed out,[1] sometimes even terrified. You ask yourself, "Am I making a mistake?"

No, you're not. As long as you protect yourself, you can safely navigate the danger zone. You must thicken your skin so that you are not oversensitive to every small slight. But at the same time you must be alert. Another betrayal may be right down the road. You need to develop body armor so that you are not left helpless if you are betrayed.

What does "being betrayed" mean to you? Everyone draws a different line. You have to develop your own standard of what you will and won't tolerate and communicate it clearly to our partner. Is any act of infidelity a betrayal? Can you overlook an occasional mini-betrayal or is it "one strike and you're out"? Will you overlook your partner's fantasizing about someone else or developing a deep emotional connection

---

[1.] Believe it or not, financial problems and economic setbacks do not cause nearly so much stress as important relationships. Dr. Frank Richardson, *Stress, Sanity, and Survival*, New York, Dutton, 1993.

as long as there is no sex? What happens if your partner has sex without intercourse with someone else? Or are you willing to accept your partner's sexual, emotional, and fantasy desires for someone else as long as he tells you the truth? Take the time to make a thoughtful decision. Whatever your standards are, stick to them. Never allow yourself to be treated disrespectfully, no matter how much you love someone.

Trust others, but not completely. *How do you find other people who are unlikely to betray you? By being honest and open yourself.* You can make a commitment to tell the truth, to communicate about what's going on with you in the present moment, and to be who you really are. Then you will attract other people on the same wavelength.

The only person you can safely trust is yourself. That's why self-sacrifice benefits no one. You give up your "self" to someone else who may, in fact, betray you. Cultivate self-love and self-trust instead. Assess your real feelings and needs, express them, and act on them. Although you can't control other people, you can control what *you* say and do.

HAVE A FALLBACK POSITION

Always give yourself a fallback position in the event that trust is violated. Don't obsess, but be ready for a crash at any time. Know how to put on your oxygen mask, don your life vest, and exit through the emergency door so you will survive in the event of a disaster. As Abby, a school teacher who was betrayed by her former husband, says to me, "I'm happily remarried now. But if he started cheating, out he'd go. I would survive. You always have to be able to stand on your own two feet if necessary. There are no guarantees." Bertha, a dental hygienist who was betrayed by her fiance, states emphatically, "Never assume that the person you love will be yours tomorrow. Love can wither away, disappear, or die. Don't get your lives so inextricably intertwined that you cannot stand alone. *Think of the people you care about most as honored guests in your life, not permanent residents.*" Say to them, "I want you in my life, but if you decide to leave I'll manage."

It is dangerous to depend completely on someone else to fill all your needs. You are connecting *with* love, not *from* love. You dance the "pleaser" dance, trying to do everything right so you don't lose your "Santa Claus." If your partner betrays you, the bottom falls out of your world. You have lost sexual pleasure, financial support, and emotional nurturing. How much safer you are if you can fill some of these needs yourself instead of relying entirely on an outside source! If you're betrayed, you can deal with it and carry on.

You and your partner aren't twins. You're two different people living two separate lives. Especially when you have children, you should always be able to survive on your own. *For healthy trust to develop you must be financially, emotionally, sexually, and spiritually independent.* Have your feet solidly planted on the ground. You'll still stand strong no matter what happens. Develop a life plan that is uniquely yours. Earn your own living; be able to support yourself. Have your own interests and your own activities. Keep in touch with friends and family. Reserve time alone to take care of your body, to pursue your hobbies, and to nourish your spirit. As you develop your independence you will become more attractive to your partner.

It's difficult to maintain your freedom within a relationship. Before you know it, you may find yourself sliding into dependency. Assess your resources from time to time. Are you making your own money? Are there other people you can talk to besides your partner when you are upset? Do you allow yourself to feel sexual desire for someone outside your relationship even if you do not express it?

At any point in time, your romantic or sexual partner can pull out the rug from under you. That's what I learned from my two mega-betrayals. The first time I almost didn't make it because I invested everything in my relationship with Charles. I had abandoned my career, my family, my friends, and my own self. The second time I was wise enough to hold onto all four of them. As St. Louis psychologist Dr. Helen Friedman wisely puts it, *"The real test is if you can say to yourself, 'If my relationship ended tonight I would still be okay.'"*[2]

Are You "Betrayal-Prone?"

Do you unconsciously encourage betrayals? Do you tend to attract people who habitually violate your trust? Carolyn, a stockbroker, tells me, "Every man I get involved with betrays me. I trust someone, he breaks my heart, and then I go out and meet the same kind of person again. I

[2.] Conversations with the author, June 21, 1996.

don't know why." Carolyn is "betrayal-prone." If this problem is deeply rooted in her past, she may need to see a therapist to find out why she's a "lousy picker." Or if she is insightful and this pattern has recently begun, she may be able to change it herself.

Carolyn is attracted to men who habitually betray. I call these people "serial betrayers." Loving them is a torment. When they betray you it is a blessing in disguise. Serial betrayers can be easily recognized because they:

- *Lie to you outright*
- *Manipulate you*
- *Play tricks on you*
- *Fail to give you important information about themselves*
- *Conceal their doings—especially those you won't approve of*
- *Treat you as objects and use you for their own purposes*

When you first meet someone, watch out for these warning signs. Serial betrayers are often charming and are usually very fast talkers. Sometimes their dishonesty is compulsive; sometimes it is a conscious choice. In either case, they destroy trust. Until your intuition screams, "Trust this person"—or you get well acquainted—treat them with caution.

BE YOUR OWN DETECTIVE

How do you know if someone you meet is a serial betrayer? Certainly he is not about to admit it to you.

First, observe your new friend's behavior carefully when you're out together. Is he telling you lies, neglecting to share vital personal information, and changing the subject when you confront? Elizabeth weeps as she tells me her story. "When I first met Derek we had marvelous chemistry. So it took me a while to figure out that there were many things he wasn't telling me. For example, we dated on Friday nights, but he'd never say exactly where he was on Saturdays or Sundays. When I'd ask him to spend more time with me he'd say, 'I have plans.' Finally, one Friday night he left me alone in his apartment. His diary was lying on his dresser. I picked it up and started to read it. 'Saturday night, dinner with Franny. Sunday afternoon, picnic with Gloria. Sunday evening, movie and sex with Isabel.' It read like a who's who of the local female scene. I admit it was terrible what I did, but at least I knew the truth. Of course I stopped seeing Derek, but I still miss him terribly. "

Check out your new friend's relationship history. Ask questions: "Why did your marriage end? How many serious relationships have you had? What went wrong?" If you don't get answers that satisfy you, discreetly ask his family, friends, and colleagues.

What about snooping? You can run the gamut from reading diaries (as Elizabeth did), going through pockets, listening in on phone conversations, going into his computer, following him, or hiring a private investigator. Draw your own line. I don't advocate snooping as a general practice, but if there's no other way to find out what you need to know, then the choice is yours.

When you move to a city full of strangers, you may meet new friends through personal ads. The person you're infatuated with may have a pattern of spousal abuse, a former wife and children in another state, or even a prior criminal record. What are you supposed to do? Give every date a lie detector test? Ask him for evidence to document everything he tells you? No. Enjoy the evening. Start from a place of trust even if it's guarded. Especially during the first few months stay awake, aware, and lovingly suspicious. Protect yourself sexually, financially, and emotionally. Insist that a condom be used when you have sex. Don't volunteer how much money you have in your personal bank account. Postpone sharing information that might be used against you, such as your ex-husband's accusation of your mental instability.

If you eventually decide to get married, should you conduct a premarital investigation? I don't think so. Hiring a private investigator can destroy trust irrevocably if your partner finds out. It is much healthier for you to take the time to get to know him well before you tie the knot. If you're worried about protecting property acquired before the two of you met, draw up a prenuptial agreement well in advance of your wedding day. If it is executed with mutual, voluntary consent, a prenuptial can actually enhance trust.

DON'T BECOME A "WALKING WOUNDED"

If Carolyn does not change her pattern herself or with help from a therapist, she may eventually become what I call a "walking wounded." These are people who have been betrayed so often that they don't trust anyone. They hide their vulnerability beneath a gruff exterior and appear cynical and defensive when you reach out. Their message is, "What's the use of having a relationship? I'm just going to be betrayed again. " They've tried and executed a potential partner before he's even committed a crime. *Don't let this happen to you.*

HAVE FAITH IN FAITH

Yes, you can trust again. I have done so, and so have hundreds of people I have met while writing this book. As *A Course in Miracles*® tells us, "Only love is real." That's the only truth there is. Betrayal and mistrust emanate from fear. The only way to live lovingly is to have faith in yourself, in other people, and in faith itself.

The Reverend Suji Hochenauer, a Unity Church minister, has composed this prayer for people who have been betrayed. Along with my own personal prayers, I offer it to you:

> Heavenly Mother/Father, let the love, joy, and peace that are part of You become manifest in [*your name*] as she moves through the storm to a safe shore and the beginning of a new life. Let [*your name*] learn to love herself and feel the love and support of the many other people who care for her and are with her in spirit. Give [*your name*] the strength to deal with whatever difficulties befall her and the faith to know that the best is yet to come."[3]

Always remember, people leave but love doesn't leave.

[3.] Reverend Suji Hochenauer, phone interview with the author, March 15, 1996.

Appendix A

Trust Meditation

I highly recommend you (and your partner, if he's willing) say the following meditation at some point while you're restoring trust. I wrote it especially for my seminar attendees. You may want to repeat it regularly until the words become embedded in your unconscious minds, or, you may wish to write your own meditation based on this model. The meditation works best when you play "Here and Never Found," a song from Ray Lynch's album *Deep Breakfast* (Ray Lynch Productions, P.O. Box 150252, San Rafael, California, 94915), in the background.

> I will make a decision right now to trust the person I love. I will do my best to keep my promises and ask my lover to do the same. I will be there for my lover when he needs me, and I will have faith that my lover will be there for me. I will trust myself; I will trust my lover.
>
> With compassion for my lover's sensitivities, I will tell him the truth. I will not pretend to be someone I am not. I will not hide important parts of me. I will share my real self and my real feelings the best I can. I will be kind to my lover when he reveals his real self to me. I will not deliberately hurt, use, abuse, control, judge, humiliate, or take advantage of my lover. I will do my best to create a comfortable, safe space where we can both reveal our faults and our sensitivities without feeling put down. I will be open with my lover and invite my lover to be open with me.

I know that sometimes I will feel betrayed or disappointed. When this happens, I will feel angry. While I am feeling angry, I may attack, blame, shame, or hurt my lover. But I also know that when my angry feelings diminish—as they inevitably will—I will forgive my lover and ask for forgiveness. My love energy is always more powerful than my attack energy.

If your partner is participating with you, take his hand. Say aloud in unison, "My love energy is always more powerful than my attack energy." Repeat several times, if you wish.

Feel the love moving from one hand to the other, like an electric current, as you stand together. Feel the love and compassion emanating from yourself.

After you do this meditation, reassess your relationship. Spend some time alone interpreting how you feel, or, if your partner is with you, share your feelings with each other.

Appendix B

Forgiveness Meditation

*D*o the following exercise together with your betrayer, if possible—especially if you intend to take him back. This meditation works best when you play "Drifted in a Deeper Land," a song from Ray Lynch's album *Deep Breakfast* (Ray Lynch Productions, P.O. Box 150252, San Rafael, California, 94915) in the background.

Sit very, very quietly and close your eyes. Breathe deeply, in-out/in-out. Say the following words together:

If I forgive you, God will bless us both.
When I feel afraid, you feel afraid.
If I attack you, you attack me back.
But if I forgive you, you forgive me.
Jesus said, "Forgive them, Lord, they know not what they do."
I myself have done—or might have done—the very same thing
    under the same circumstances.
What is most important is our holy relationship.
I choose not to dwell on the past; my power is the present moment.
Let me focus on what is good, the god or goddess within you.
I choose to overlook your mistake because I see your greater goodness.
As I celebrate your beauty, I celebrate my own.
I'm sorry for not being there for you, for not understanding you,
    for attacking you, for accusing you, for ignoring how you feel,
    or for forgetting what you need.
I'll do it differently next time, I promise I will.
Whatever I've done, whatever I've said, I'll make it up to you. I
    promise I will, I promise I will, *I promise I will. I promise I will.*

BETRAYED!

Let's remember how close we really are.
Our love can grow stronger as we make amends.
Our love grows as we make amends.
Our love grows as we make amends.
Our love grows as we make amends.

I forgive you for what you've said or done.
I accept the amends you're making right now.
Forgiveness is a gift for you; forgiveness is a gift for me.
Forgiveness lets us both be free to love each other again.
Forgiveness is to love again, to love again, to love again, *to love each other again.*

I'm sorry for not being there for you, for not understanding you, for attacking you, for accusing you, for ignoring how you feel, or for forgetting what you need.
I'll do it differently next time, I promise I will.
Whatever I've done, whatever I've said, I'll make it up to you. I promise I will.

I forgive you for what you've said or done.
I accept the amends you're making right now.
I forgive you for what you've said or done
I accept the amends you're making right now.
Forgiveness is a gift for you; forgiveness is a gift for me.
Forgiveness lets us both be free to love each other again.
To love each other again.
To love each other again.

Appendix C

Recommended Books and Tapes

Books

Amodeo, John. 1994. *Love and Betrayal: Broken Trust in Intimate Relationships*. New York: Ballentine Books.

Blanton, Brad. 1996. *Radical Honesty: How to Transform Your Life by Telling the Truth*. New York: Dell Publishing.

Burnell, Ivan. 1997. *Say Yes to Life*. Center Ossipee, NH: I.P.D. Publishing.

Fisher, Bruce. 1992. *Rebuilding: When Your Relationship Ends*. San Luis Obispo, CA: Impact Publishers.

Hay, Louise. 1988. *Heal Your Body*. Revised Edition. Carlsbad, CA: Hay House.

Jones, Riki Robbins. 1992. *The Empowered Woman*, New York, SPI Books.

Jones, Riki Robbins, 1995. *Negotiating Love: How Women and Men Can Resolve Their Differences*, New York, Ballantine Books.

Klein, Marty. 1990. *Your Sexual Secrets: When to Keep Them, How to Share Them*. New York: Berkley Books.

Morin, Jack. 1996. *The Erotic Mind: Unlocking the Inner Sources of Sexual Passion and Fulfillment*. New York: HarperPerennial.

Schucman, Helen, and William Thetford. 1975. *A Course in Miracles®*. Mill Valley, CA: Foundation for Inner Peace, Inc.

Sherven, Judith, and James Sniechowski. 1997. *The New Intimacy: Finding the Passion at the Heart of Your Differences*. Deerfield Beach, Florida: Health Communications, Inc.

Trafford, Abigail. 1992. *Crazy Time: Surviving Divorce and Building a New Life.* Revised Edition. New York: HarperPerennial.

Vaughan, Diane. 1990. *Uncoupling: Turning Points in Intimate Relationships.* New York: Vintage Books.

Tapes

Broer, Eileen. 1997. "The Power of Unfinished Business." Cary, NC: Human Dimensions.

Farrell, Warren. 1992. "Understanding Each Other." Boulder, CO: Sounds True Recordings.

Johnson, Jack. 1995. "Male Multiple Orgasm." Third Edition. Ashland, OR: Jack Johnston Seminars.

Swack, Judith. 1997. "Love Phobia." Needham, MA: Judith A. Swack & Associates.

INDEX
∽∽

A
abandonment, 18, 31, 32, 100
acceptance
  emotional, 20, 87-88
  of responsibility, 26
accomplice
  analysis of, 44-46, 47, 48-50
  comparisons with, 26
  forgiveness for, 156-157
  rationalization by, 46-47
  "serial accomplice", 46
  support provided by, 42, 68
advice, recommendations for, 108-109
affirmations. *see also* healthy voice
  for recovery, 14-17, 18, 19, 20, 21, 89-90
  for self-empowerment, 49
  for self-love, 86, 87
anger. *see also* emotions; rage
  about accomplice, 48
  effect on partners, 4, 7, 127-128
  overcoming, 7, 19, 21, 48, 110
  as warning sign, 51-52

B
betrayal
  components of, 3, 50-60
  mega/mini-betrayal, 32, 88, 123, 161
  of oneself, 27
  origins for, 63-82
  preparing for, 6, 8, 119, 128, 149
  real vs. perceived, 32-33
  recognizing, 27-28, 34
  ten ways to overcome, 4-5
betrayal prevention, prescription for, 80-81
"betrayal-prone" personality, 163-164
betrayer
  breaking bond with, 99-100, 149-150
  communication with, 4, 9, 15, 33, 99-100, 124-125
  confronting, 53-55, 56-60, 124
  forgiveness for, 156-157, 158
  information about, 25, 52, 56-58, 80, 164-165
  portrait of, 35, 81-82
  "serial betrayer", 163-165
  taking back after betrayal, 30, 143-150, 158
black flags, watching out for, 51-52, 58-59, 82, 126, 139
blame, 26, 41, 110
boundaries, 43
breakup
  secrecy affecting, 29
  sudden, compared to resolved, 4, 7

C
Callahan Method, 139
change
  emotional, 51-52, 67, 78, 82
  factors affecting, 120
  in lifestyle, 52, 66, 73, 78, 95-98
  in sexual behavior, 51, 78, 87, 96
  unacknowledged, 66-67, 77-78, 81
  as warning indicator, 51-52

cheating, 27-30. *see also* betrayal
children. *see also* family; parenting
  betrayal affecting, 9, 112-113, 147
  communicating with, 59
  support provided by, 4
choice
  force of in betrayal, 63-64, 82
  for trust, 119
communication
  with betrayer, 4, 9, 15, 33, 99-100, 124-125
  boundaries affecting, 43, 77, 79
  in breakup process, 7, 54-55, 81-82, 99-100
  of emotional pain, 20-21
  of emotions, 20-21, 55, 56-60, 101, 106-107,
    124-125, 127, 158
  fear affecting, 44
  inspirational, 93-94
  for sexual trust, 30, 78-79, 137-139
confession, 59-60
confrontation, with betrayer, 53-55, 56-60, 124
confusion, 42
control
  enhancement of, 4
  loss of, 16, 18, 120
counseling. *see* therapy
A Course in Miracles, 7, 37, 89
crying, 18
cybersex, 30, 68, 76, 79, 136. *see also* fantasy

D
"danger zone", 161-162
death, as abandonment, 31
denial
  discussed, 50, 51-53
  effect on betrayed, 4, 54
  overcoming, 52-53, 58
desperation, 110
  of betrayer, 64, 73, 75
diet, 90-91
disease. *see also* health; physical ailments
  affecting betrayer, 42, 43
  prevention of, 5, 6, 17, 120, 128, 134, 149, 165
  as reason for betrayal, 27
divorce
  as betrayal, 28, 31
  process of, 99-100
domestic violence
  as betrayal, 28, 31
  fear of, 54
"the drink," 91

E
ego, emotions affecting, 17, 49, 66, 75-76
embarrassment. *see* shame
emotions. *see also* anger
  acceptance of, 20, 87-88, 91, 163
  after betrayal, 145
  changes in, 51-52, 67, 78, 82
  communicating, 4, 10, 20-21, 55, 56-60, 101,
    107, 124-125, 127, 158

BETRAYED!

disconnection of, 69-70, 79
five waves of, 14, 32
outrage, 19-20
rage, 19, 21
sadness, 18-19
self-destructive forces in, 41-42
shame, 17-18
shock, 15-17
suppressed, 64-80, 79, 88
The Empowered Woman (Robbins), 6
entitlement, 72-73, 154
exercise, 90-91
explanation, 4, 9. *see also* information

F

faith. *see also* prayer; spirituality
enhancement of, 7
in oneself, 21, 166
as positive resource, 5, 92
questioning of, 16
in relationship partner, 29, 119
fallback position, 119, 162-163
family. *see also* children
betrayal affecting, 45, 101, 105
betrayal by, 111-112
communicating with, 106
support provided by, 4, 7, 14, 25, 92, 97, 98
support recommendations for, 107-111
trust in, 121-122
fantasy
as cheating, 28
fulfillment of, 68, 96, 129, 134-135
unfulfillment of, 66, 76, 77-78, 120, 133
fear
compared to love, 37-38, 70, 95, 119-120, 161-162
experienced by betrayed, 49, 54, 81, 109
experienced by betrayer, 43, 44
overcoming, 85, 129, 139, 158
feelings. *see* emotions
financial issues, 5, 9, 87, 93, 97, 120, 147, 163, 165
career choices, 95, 109
financial security, as positive resource, 4, 90, 91
flirting, 120
forgiveness, 19, 30, 92, 146
recommendations for, 153-158
freedom
after betrayal, 86, 163
sought by betrayer, 72, 73-74
friends
betrayal affecting, 105
betrayal by, 111-112
communicating with, 106
support provided by, 4, 7, 8, 14, 25, 55, 59, 60, 92, 97, 98
support recommendations for, 107-111
friendship
enhancement of, 96, 149
provided by accomplice, 68
and sexual trust, 137
fun, 109

G

gifts, 107-108
grief, 42
growth
factors affecting, 49
in recovery, 21, 100-101, 150
guilt
of accomplice, 47
overcoming, 41, 53

H

Heal Your Body (Hay), 99
healing. *see also* forgiveness
for emotional release, 55, 56-60, 113
health. *see also* disease; physical ailments
diet and exercise affecting, 90-91, 92-93
emotional release affecting, 55, 56-60
as positive resource, 4, 5, 90-91
sought by betrayer, 74
healthy voice. *see also* affirmations
affirmations for enhancing, 14-17, 18, 19, 20, 21
honesty. *see also* truth
compared to lying, 36-37, 128-129
in recovery, 87, 126, 136, 138, 162
sought by betrayer, 78
hopelessness, 17-18, 44
humiliation, 44, 54
hypocrisy, 36

I

independence, 163
information. *see also* questions
about betrayer, 25, 56-58, 80
about partners, 134
for children, 113
for family and friends, 106
from betrayer, 52, 164-165
and trust, 122, 123, 128, 165
inner strength. *see also* resources
realization of, 89-91
innocence, and responsibility, 26
inspiration, 4, 8, 93
integrity
factors affecting, 41, 60, 118, 121, 126, 146
and loyalty, 35, 46
intimacy
enhancement of, 129, 137
sought by betrayer, 65, 69-70
intuition, trusting, 118-119
isolation, 4, 6

J

joy, 85, 86, 90, 146
judgement, 30

L

lies. *see also* promise-breaking
black and white lies, 35-37, 126, 128
compared to broken promises, 32
destructive force of, 59, 122, 127, 158, 164